STILL INSPIRED BY . . .

STILL INSPIRED BY . . .

By Suzanne Newman

RESOURCE *Publications* · Eugene, Oregon

STILL INSPIRED BY . . .

Copyright © 2025 Suzanne Newman. All rights reserved. Except for brief quotations in critical publications or reviews, no part of this book may be reproduced in any manner without prior written permission from the publisher. Write: Permissions, Wipf and Stock Publishers, 199 W. 8th Ave., Suite 3, Eugene, OR 97401.

Resource Publications
An Imprint of Wipf and Stock Publishers
199 W. 8th Ave., Suite 3
Eugene, OR 97401

www.wipfandstock.com

PAPERBACK ISBN: 979-8-3852-5539-9
HARDCOVER ISBN: 979-8-3852-5540-5
EBOOK ISBN: 979-8-3852-5541-2

VERSION NUMBER 071025

I'd like to dedicate this book to my family,
particularly my children.

I would also like to dedicate this book in the loving memory of…
Our dearest friend Simon
(died 36 years old)
And
Grandma "Frankie"
(died 86 years old)

Both of whom died recently.

(Please note that any profits the author makes from this book will be donated to Cancer Research and Alzheimer's Research charities).

CONTENTS

Preface | xi
Introduction | xiii

Jacob's Dream | 1
The Burning Bush | 3
The First Passover | 5
Balaam's Donkey | 7
Gideon and the Fleece | 10
Samuel | 14
Elijah and the Altar | 17
The Widow's Olive Oil | 19
Nehemiah and Jerusalem's Wall | 21
Hope In Suffering | 26
Dry Bones | 28
Israel Will Rise | 30
God's Judgement Against Nineveh | 32
Following the New Star | 34
Preparing the Way | 36
Jesus Tempted In the Wilderness | 39
Treasures In Heaven | 41
The House On the Rock | 42
John the Baptist Is Beheaded | 44
Jesus Walks On Water | 46
The Transfiguration | 48
A Camel Through the Eye of A Needle | 49

The Oil Lamps of the Ten Virgins | 51
The Sheep and the Goats | 53
Denial | 56
The Man Lowered Through the Roof | 58
Legion | 61
Jesus Heals A Sick Woman | 63
His Name Is John | 65
Mary's Wonderment | 67
The Shepherds | 69
Jesus Presented In the Temple | 71
A Sinful Woman Washes Jesus's Feet | 73
The Good Samaritan | 75
Warnings and Encouragements | 77
The Rich Fool | 79
The Lost Son | 81
The Rich Man and Lazarus | 83
Jesus Heals Ten Men With Leprosy | 85
The Coming of the Kingdom of God | 86
The Pharisee and the Tax Collector | 88
Zacchaeus | 89
On the Right Side of the Christ | 91
Water Into Wine | 92
Nicodemus | 93
The Woman and the Well | 94
The Healing At the Pool | 97
Jesus Promises the Holy Spirit | 99
The Vine and the Branches | 100
Jesus Sentenced To Be Crucified | 101
Simon the Sorcerer | 103
Philip and the Ethiopian | 105
Trials and Rewards | 107
Bible Verse—Romans Ch5 V1–7 | 109

EPILOGUE | 110
Contents— | 110
Dressing Appropriately In the Dark | 111
When You're Feeling Down... | 113
The Battle For Sanity | 115
I'll Deal With the Cards I'm Dealt | 118
I Know The Truth | 120
Every Grace-Filled Breath | 122
Soul-Battery | 124
Lord, Please Re-Paint Me | 125
Persevere | 128
The Light Shows Us | 130
Nobody's Perfect | 133
Tears Travel Up | 134
I'll Be With You | 136
Bit By Bit | 138
If The Dirt Could Talk | 140

Word of *Thanks* | 144
Further Information About the Author | 145

PREFACE

This book was written after The Lord put it on my heart to pen a sequel to "Inspired By…" which was co-authored by Mr Michael Grgich and I back in 2020.

The original "Inspired By…" is a Biblically accurate poetic retelling of some of the most well-known moments in The Bible, from Genesis all the way through to Revelation, including the crucifixion and resurrection of The Lord Jesus Christ. Some-time later it struck me that there was still so much more to write about, and hence the initial stirrings of another book slowly began.

For around two years I didn't know when or even how I was going to ever start to attempt to write this! It seemed like a very daunting task at first, so I started by jotting down some of the key parts of Scripture I had always felt personally touched by. Over time this list grew, and prompted and guided by The Holy Spirit, it continued to change/expand along the way as God directed. Naturally, in time, God decided the time was right for this book to be written, and so here we are! It ended up eventually being a very natural process, which I am very grateful to The Lord for.

It was a humbling honour and privilege to be God's vessel/servant in this way. I am nothing special, and I acknowledge I am nothing without Him in all things, but particularly in this project…there's absolutely no way I could have written this without The Lord. He has moved me greatly during the creation and writing of this book and He works in marvellous and mysterious ways for sure.

I hope you will enjoy the poetic spiritual journey this book takes you on and that you will then check out The Scriptures afresh for yourselves and maybe be inspired yourself!

All glory to God…always.

INTRODUCTION

The most important point to make about this book is that it is Biblically accurate. No attempt has been made at gross poetic license, and I have in no way tried to "re-write" Scripture as we are warned about in the book of Revelation. This project is for God's glory and re-introduces the reader to His word and its wise lessons in an interesting poetic way, whilst staying true Biblically. It has been written with care and love and all due humility and reverence, acknowledging that I am merely God's grateful servant in all things.

Please note that all direct Bible quotes and references are taken from the World English Bible (WEB) which is in the public domain. I used this translation as a base for all 53 poems to ensure accuracy.

The title "Still Inspired By…" is quite self-explanatory really…
I (and indeed all of us) continue to still be inspired by God on a personal level every day and this never ends. What also never ends is the constant learning and maturing we receive via The Bible, and the wisdom, knowledge and truth held within its pages. I know I will still be inspired by The Lord and His written word for the rest of my life.

Whilst the original book "Inspired By…" took the reader on a more obvious, general, and organized journey right through from Genesis to Revelation, this second book, "Still Inspired By…", was written in a way that really spoke to me personally. Consequently, on the surface, this may seem to have much more random choices of Scripture! Starting with Jacob's dream of Heaven's staircase, Balaam's donkey and Gideon and the fleece, and ending with The Vine and the branches, Philip and the Ethiopian, and trials and rewards, with so much more in-between, "Still Inspired By…" hopes to encourage readers to marvel afresh at God's miracles, grace, wisdom and power that is revealed to us all in the pages of His written word.

Each one of the fifty-three poems in the first section of this book follows Scripture very closely, summarizes a particular Bible chapter or verse/verses and retells it in a simple poetry style that everyone can easily understand. Every piece has the corresponding passage of Scripture next to the title, so the reader can check out the Biblical accuracy for themselves. Pieces have been presented chronologically, but can be read in whatever order you like, or just as single, random individual poems. There is no set way to read this book, it's however you choose!

In the epilogue of this book, I have included a few of the "everyday" personal poems that I have become known for sharing on Facebook and in various charity anthologies. I constantly write about how God is there for us in various ways during every single struggle we ever face in our lives. I write from the heart and my own experiences about topics such as cancer, mental illness, grief etc. By sharing these it is my humble hope that others may be encouraged and reassured in their relationship with The Lord, knowing that He never leaves us to deal with things alone, because His presence, promises, grace and love are reliable and never ending.

All glory to God…always and forever.

JACOB'S DREAM

(Based on Genesis Ch28 verse 10-end of chapter).

Jacob went out from Beersheba, towards Harran,
And when he reached a certain place,
He stopped for the night and halted his pace,
Because the sun had set,
And he couldn't see where to step next.
He took one of the stones of the place,
And put it under his head,
For a pillow, and the ground then became his bed.

Whilst sleeping, Jacob had a dream,
About the most marvellous staircase ever seen,
A staircase set upon the earth,
Its top reaching Heaven, where there is no hurt,
And the angels of God were ascending,
And descending on it.

Above it all there stood Yahweh, The Lord,
Magnificent in grace and power outpoured.
He said, "I am Yahweh, and I will give to you
And your offspring, the land you're lying on.
Your offspring will be as the dust of the earth,
And you will spread out West and East and North and South,
And show your Holy worth.

Behold, I am with you and will watch over you,
And bring you again into this land,
I will not leave until I have done
What I have promised to do, by my own hand".

When Jacob awoke from his slumber,
He remembered the dream that he'd been under,
He was afraid with reverent awe,
And concluded this place did surely belong to The Lord.

Jacob arose early in the morn,
Took the stone he'd slept on the night before,
Set it up as a pillar and began to pour
Oil on top of it.
He called that place Bethel, and vowed a vow,
Saying "If God will be with me on my journey now,
And give me bread to eat and clothes to wear,
So I may come again to my father's house over there,
Then Yahweh will be my God.
And this stone that I have set,
Up as a pillar, will be God's house yet,
And of all that you'll give me,
I will give you a tenth".

THE BURNING BUSH

(Based on Exodus Ch3 verses 1–13)

Moses was tending his father-in-law Jethro's flock,
He led them over the wilderness to Horeb,
And came to a mountain of God,
There the angel of The Lord did appear to him,
In the flames of a bush, which was on fire within.
Moses saw the bush was ablaze, but was not consumed,
He was curious and a little bemused,
And when he went over to look, the voice of God
Called out to him,
"Moses! Moses!" from the middle within.

And Moses replied, "Here I am".
"Do not come close," God said.
"Take off your sandals, for the place you are standing
On is Holy ground".
Moses hid his face…he didn't look up or around,
For he was afraid to look at God,
Who said, "I am the God of your father,
The God of Abraham,
The God of Isaac, and the God of Jacob".

Yahweh explained
That He had seen the misery and pain

Of His people in Egypt, under their taskmaster's reign.
He was concerned about their suffering,
So had come down to rescue them and to bring
Them out of The Egyptian's hands,
Into a new, good and spacious land,
Flowing with milk at honey at His command.
"So now, go. . .
I am sending you to Pharaoh,
To bring my people, the children of Israel, out of Egypt".

"But who am I Lord?" Moses asked,
"To undertake such a great, grand task!"
"I will be with you", God reassured.
And you cannot fail when you do the work of The Lord.

THE FIRST PASSOVER

(Based on Exodus Ch12 verses 1–15)

In Egypt, Yahweh gave Moses and Aaron
Strict instructions regarding preparing the lamb
In every household in the community of Israel,
So The Lord's first Passover plan wouldn't fail.

When the lambs were slaughtered,
People were to take some blood,
And put it on the doorframes of their houses -
On the two door posts and the lintel above,
And that night they must eat the meat,
Roasted over the fire,
As per The Lord's desire,
With bitter herbs and bread made without yeast.
And The Lord said, "This is how you shall eat –
With your belt on your waist and sandals on your feet,
Staff in your hand,
And eat in haste,
No time to waste,
For it is Yahweh's Passover.

On that same night I will go through,
And strike down every first-born man and animal within view,
And execute judgement against all the gods of Egypt.

"I am Yahweh".
And the blood that you've poured
And marked your houses with,
Will be the sign that I will pass over you,
And no destructive plague will be on or destroy you,
When I strike the land of Egypt.

And this day shall be a memorial for you,
To commemorate,
For generations to come you shall celebrate
It as a festival to The Lord,
A lasting ordinance, with one accord".

BALAAM'S DONKEY

(Based on Numbers Ch22 verses 21–36)

Balaam rose up in the morning, saddled his donkey,
And went off with the princes of Moab.
God's anger burned because he went,
And Yahweh's angel stood, Heaven-sent,
On the path, as an adversary against him.
Balaam was riding his donkey,
And the donkey veered off course
When he looked and saw,
God's angel standing in the road,
With his hand out, holding his large sword drawn.

The donkey turned into a field,
But Balaam struck her to get her back on track,
And as they went through the vineyard's narrow path,
The angel of the Lord came back.
When the donkey saw the angel,
She thrust herself in to the vineyard's wall,
Thus crushing Balaam's foot,
So he struck the donkey again, not understanding at all.

Then the angel went further...
And stood in a narrow place,
That had nowhere to turn, left or right, for there was no space,
And when the donkey saw the angel,

She laid down under Balaam.
Balaam's anger burned,
And so he turned
And struck the donkey, with his staff.
Then God opened-up her mouth.
Imagine Balaam's shock and surprise,
When the donkey looked at him and words came out!

"What have I done to you, that you have struck me these three times?"
Balaam answered, "Because you have mocked me!
If I had a sword in my hand, I would kill you,
Here and now, quite happily and readily."
The donkey replied, "Am I not your donkey,
On which you have ridden all your life until day?
Have I ever been in the habit of doing this to you,
Or been disobedient in any way?"
"No", said Balaam.
And then Yahweh opened Balaam's ignorant eyes,
Who saw the angel, sword drawn,
Standing on the roadside.
So Balaam bowed down low and fell face down,
And in reverence waited, humbly, upon the ground.

"Why have you struck your donkey these three times?"
The angel of Yahweh asked.
"Behold, I have come out as an adversary,
Because your way is perverse before me,
The donkey saw me and turned away,
Three times, but if she hadn't done,
Surely now I would have killed you,
And saved her alive",
The angel's warning rung.

Balaam said, "I have sinned, for I did not know
That you stood in the way against me, in the middle of the road.
Now therefore, if it displeases you,
I will go back again".
And he awaited instructions on what he should do.
"Go with the men", the angel said,
To Balaam, who was bowing his head,
"But you shall only speak the word that I shall speak to you."
So Balaam went with the princes of Balak,
Now obedient and faithful, with an enlightened view.

GIDEON AND THE FLEECE

(Based on Judges Ch6—whole chapter).

Because they did evil in His eyes,
The Lord gave the Israelites
Into the hands of the oppressive Midianites,
For seven years.

The brutal Midianites would never spare
A single thing for the Israelites where
They'd planted crops.
The Midianites came up with their livestock,
And tents, like swarms of destructive locusts,
Invading land just to ravage it, making a fuss,
Until the children of Israel could cope no more,
And desperately cried out to The Lord.

So Yahweh sent them a prophet to explain,
The reason for their suffering and current pain -
He said that Yahweh had brought them out
From Egypt and that cruel bondage-house,
Delivered them out of their oppressor's hand,
Driving them out and giving His people that land.
Yahweh had told them loud and clear
Not to fear
The gods of the Amorites,
But they would not hear,
And didn't listen to His Almighty voice.

Then Yahweh's angel came, and sat and spoke,
To a man called Gideon, underneath an oak,
Where Gideon was busy beating out wheat
In a winepress, in order that he could keep
And hide it from the Midianites.
The angel said, "Yahweh is with you, you mighty man of valor!"

The Lord then explained to Gideon, who was confused,
That He was sending him to save Israel from the abuse
It suffered at the Midianite's hands.
Gideon didn't really understand,
How HE could be the one to save,
For his clan was weak,
And he himself was least
In his family.

The Lord answered, "Surely I will be with you,
And you will strike the Midianites, as one man".
Gideon replied,
"Please send me a sign,
That you really are The Lord Divine,
And it IS you who talks and walks with me.
Please don't go away until I come to you,
And bring out my present, and lay it before you".
So Yahweh agreed,
To wait,
As per Gideon's plea.

So Gideon went off,
And prepared meat, unleavened bread, and broth in a pot,
And brought them as an offering under the oak,
Where the angel of The Lord once more spoke,
And instructed Gideon to put them on a rock.
He then got his sign, and quite a shock,

When the angel used his staff-end to cause
A fire flare,
Consuming the meat and the bread in the name of The Lord.

The angel then disappeared,
And Gideon realized, in excitement and reverent fear,
That he had just seen an angel of Yahweh face to face!
But The Lord said, "Peace be to you! Don't be afraid.
You shall not die".
So Gideon put his fears aside,
Then built an alter there for all to see,
And praise God, and called it, "Yahweh is peace".

That same night, The Lord told Gideon
To tear down his father's altar,
That he'd built to Baal, and do not falter,
Then build a proper altar to Yahweh—me,
And Gideon followed God's instructions faithfully.

In the morning, the townsfolk were so annoyed,
And told Joash to bring his boy—
His son, Gideon,
To pay for what he'd done.
They said, "He must die",
But Joash defied,
And said, "If Baal really is a god,
He can defend himself when someone breaks down his altar".
So, the townsfolk decided to let Baal contend
With Gideon and his servant men.

Meanwhile, Gideon further tested God
About His promise of saving Israel by his hand. . .
"I will place a wool-fleece on the threshing floor,
And if the ground is dry at morn,
But only on the fleece there's dew,

Then I will know that what you've said is true".
That is what happened—
Gideon rose to find
Only the fleece was soaked,
And the ground, bone dry.

Then Gideon said, "Don't be angry, Lord,
I made a request, can I make one more?
This time please let the fleece be dry,
And the ground covered with dew,
Then I'll know it's you,
And what you've said is true".
That night God did exactly this—
The ground was wet with dew,
But bone dry was the woollen-fleece.

SAMUEL

(Based on 1 Samuel Ch1 & Ch3 - whole chapters)

A man named Elkanah had two wives—
Peninnah, who had children,
And Hannah who had none, so she cried,
Because The Lord had closed her womb inside.
Peninnah teased and provoked poor Hannah
Because she was barren,
To the point where Hannah would not eat,
Elkanah was concerned, for he loved Hannah best,
And hated to see her grieve and weep.

In deep anguish, Hannah prayed to The Lord,
Her desperate tears making her cheeks sore,
And she made a vow,
To God right now,
Saying if He would let her have a son,
She'd give him to The Lord
For all the days of his life,
And no razor would ever be used on his head, she swore.

Eli the priest observed her mouth,
Which was moving, but no voice came out,
So he thought her drunk!
He told her to put away the wine,
But she explained she was pouring out no wine,

Just her heart and soul out to The Lord Divine.
"Don't consider your servant a wicked woman;
For I have been speaking out of the abundance of my complaint and my provocation".
Eli answered, "Go in peace,
And may the God of Israel grant your petition that you have asked of Him".
Hannah was encouraged and no longer downcast,
And went away to eat something, at last.

The next morning, they arose and worshipped before The Lord,
Then returned to their home at Ramah.
Elkanah made love to his wife Hannah,
And God graciously remembered her,
And in due course she became pregnant.
She gave birth to a healthy son,
She named him Samuel, saying
"Because I have asked Yahweh for him,
And behold the miracle He has done".

The boy Samuel, after he was weaned,
Was given to The Lord, as Hannah vowed it would be,
And he went into the care of Eli the priest.

In those days, the word of The Lord was rare,
And not many visions ever appeared there.
One night, Eli had gone to bed,
When twice Samuel rushed into him and said,
"Here I am; you called me".
Eli said, "I did not call—go back and lie down".
Samuel was perplexed and frowned his brow.
It happened a second and third time,
Before Eli finally realized,

The call was actually from The Lord.
Eli told Samuel to open his ears,
And be of good cheer,
"If God calls you again, say
'Speak, Yahweh; for your servant hears".
So Samuel went back and lay in his place,
Waiting for The Lord's voice to come in that space.

And The Lord spoke to Samuel,
Saying He was about
To do something to Israel,
And at that time He would carry out
Everything against Eli and his family He spoke about. . .
He told Eli He would judge his family
Because of the iniquity which He knew about,
And that the guilt of Eli's house
Will never be atoned for
By any sacrifice or offering
They might bring.

Samuel was afraid the next morn
To tell Eli this message, sent from The Lord,
But Eli insisted.
Samuel hid nothing from him,
And told him everything.
Eli replied,
"It is Yahweh. Let Him do what seems good to Him."
The Lord was with Samuel as he grew,
And all of Israel recognized and knew
That Samuel was
Attested as a prophet of God.

ELIJAH AND THE ALTAR

(Based on 1 Kings Ch18 verses 22–40).

Elijah addressed the people and said,
"I am the only one of The Lord's prophets left,
But Baal has four hundred and fifty prophets".
So Elijah set up a test. . .
He told them to get two bulls,
And Baal's prophets would get to choose one,
And he would take the other one.
The meat would be prepared by them,
Put on the wood, but not set a fire, and then
They'd call upon the name of each god,
And the one who answers by fire. . .well, He then is God.
Everyone agreed and was keen to see.

Baal's prophets called upon his name
From morning 'til noon, but there came no flame,
No smoke, no response,
From their so-called god.
As they leaped around the altar they'd made,
Elijah taunted them, laughing at Baal's 'great' name,
Suggesting maybe he was busy or sleeping!
The prophets shouted louder, slashed themselves until
Their blood was flowing, and on the ground spilled.

Midday passed and they continued on,
Until the time for evening sacrifice had come and gone,
But still there was not a single response
From their so-called god.

Then Elijah said to the people to come to him,
As he repaired the torn-down altar of The Lord,
Arranged the wood and prepared the bull,
And told them to get four large jars full
Of water, and pour them all upon
The offering and the wood…
And so it was done.
Three times over this occurred,
So there was no physical way an ordinary fire could burn.

At the time of sacrifice, Elijah stepped forward,
Praying to The God of Abraham, Isaac and Israel, and calling Him Lord,
And asked Him to show the people who
He is and just what He can do,
To prove HE is The only one God who is true.

Then the fire of The Almighty Lord
Came down and Holy flames did roar,
Burning up the sacrificial meat,
The wood, the stones, the soil,
And even the trench-water at their feet!
When the people saw, they cried out in awe,
And acknowledged THIS God was indeed THE Lord.

THE WIDOW'S OLIVE OIL

(Based on 2 Kings Ch4 verses 1–8).

A woman cried out to Elisha—
"Your servant my husband is dead.
You know that he revered The Lord,
But now his creditor comes tomorrow morn
To take my two boys as his slaves".
Elisha asked her how he could help out,
And exactly what she had left in her house. . .
"Nothing" she sadly replied,
"Except a small pot of oil inside".

Elisha told her to go around
All her neighbors,
And ask for any empty jars that could be found,
Not just a few, but lots and lots,
And then go inside with all she'd got,
With her two sons and shut the door,
Get the olive oil and begin to pour
It into each and every jar.

She did this, and then said to her son,
"All the jars are full. . .bring me another one",
But he replied "There's no more left!
No more clay jars. . .we are bereft".
Only then did the oil stop flowing.

She went and told the man of God,

Who said to go and sell the oil,

To pay off all her debts,

And then she and her sons could live off the rest of the spoils.

NEHEMIAH AND JERUSALEM'S WALL

(Based on Nehemiah Ch2 verse 11—Ch7 verse 4).

Nehemiah went to Jerusalem,
And had not told anyone
What God had put on his heart,
By night he went through the Valley Gate,
Examining Jerusalem's walls, and from the start
He noticed they had been broken down,
And its gates destroyed with fire.
The officials did not know what Nehemiah was doing,
Or the intended work that he and God desired.

In time, Nehemiah said to everyone,
"Let's rebuild the wall,
And no longer will we be in disgrace",
He also told them that God's hand was on him,
So they could not fail, and his plan picked up pace.
They were mocked and ridiculed by the opposition,
But Nehemiah stood firm in his faithful position,
"The God of Heaven will give us success", he said,
"As for you, you have no share or claim
Or historic right to Jerusalem".

Eliashib and his fellow priests
Went to work on the gate known as The Sheep,

The men of Jericho built the adjoining section,
And Zakkur, son of Imri, built next to them.
The Fish Gate was then rebuilt by
The sons of Hassenaah,
Who laid beams, bolts and bars.
The many sections after this
Were all repaired and rebuilt,
And no workers were remiss.

Goldsmiths, perfume-makers and traders
All worked hard on this restoration,
Past The Broad Wall and The Tower of Ovens,
Even Shallum's daughters helped repair the devastation.
The Valley Gate, The Dung Gate,
And over a thousand cubits of Jerusalem's wall,
Were lovingly repaired and restored,
All under the hand of The Almighty Lord.

The Fountain Gate was repaired by Shallun—
Son of the ruler of the district of Mizpah,
He roofed it over and put on doors, and bolts and bars.
Beyond him, Nehemiah—son of Azbuk,
Made repairs right up to opposite the tombs,
Next to him, The Levites set to work,
And priests, and merchants, and temple servants,
And men of Tekoa picked up tools and brooms. . .
A labour of love,
To obey the will of God.

The work on the wall quickly progressed,
But when Sanballat heard, he became angry and greatly incensed,
And he ridiculed the Jews.

Still they rebuilt the wall,
For they worked at it with all
Their heart,
Until every bit was half its height in every part.
But the Arabs and the Ammonites
And the people of Ashdod didn't think it right,
And became angry as the gaps were closed,
And plotted together to fight it and it posed
A very real threat.
But the Jews prayed to God,
And posted guard day and night,
And Nehemiah still trusted it would all be alright.

But their enemies planned to plant themselves in the midst
Of the workers, so they'd have no chance to resist,
Or defend themselves when their foes attacked quick,
And then they would be killed. . .
Thus putting an end to the work and belittling their God's will.
The Jews were fearful of attack,
From their enemies lurking behind their backs,
Therefore, Nehemiah stationed people behind
The lowest points of the wall, and gave them supplies
Of swords and spears and bows,
So they could defend themselves from the enemy's blows,
Whenever their evil plot was exposed.
"Don't be afraid", Nehemiah reminded them,
"Remember The Lord is more powerful than these men,
And when we fight, we don't fight alone,
So fight for your families, your wives and homes".
The enemies heard that God had frustrated their plan,
And The Jews returned to working on the wall with zealous hands.

From that day onwards, half the men did the workmanship,
While the other half were well-equipped
With armour, shields and bows and spears—
Prepared for if their foes came near.
And each builder wore his sword at his side,
But the man with the trumpet stayed beside Nehemiah,
Who said, "Because the work on this wall is very spread out,
Whenever you hear the trumpet sound out,
Come and join us here.
Our God will fight for us!"

Further opposition to the rebuild of the wall kept coming,
But because God was with them, nobody went running.
The enemy schemed to harm Nehemiah,
Who four times said no,
When they suggested a meeting in a village in Ono.
They continued to frighten the workers, and thought
That their hands would get weak
And so not complete
The wall as they ought.
But Nehemiah prayed
That things wouldn't be this way,
And asked God to strengthen hands.

Despite all the intimidation, schemes, and lies,
Nehemiah didn't sin, didn't run away, or hide,
And diligently, in the name and the strength of The Lord,
Work WAS completed on Jerusalem's wall,
In no time at all...
Just fifty-two days!

When the enemies heard about this,
All their self-confidence was dismissed
And lost,
For they now were afraid of this unstoppable God.
The surrounding nations were also afraid,
When they realized that the wall's progress had been made
According to God's will.

After the wall was rebuilt,
And all the doors were in place,
The gatekeepers, musicians,
And the Levites were appointed their place.
Men of integrity were to be in charge,
Including Nehemiah's brother—Hanani,
Who had instructions not to open the gates
Until the sun was hot and high enough in the sky.
The gatekeepers, whilst still on duty,
Were to shut the doors and bar them,
And also appointed to be guards,
Were some local residents of Jerusalem.

***

To restore Jerusalem's wall,
In The name of The Lord. . .
This task was huge,
This task was vast,
But the work got done,
And it got done fast,
For each worker there
Worked from the heart.
And no foe on earth can ever stop
The work that is done according to the will of God.

HOPE IN SUFFERING

(Based on Lamentations Ch3 verses 1–34).

I am the man who has seen affliction by the rod of God's wrath.
He has driven me away,
And made me walk down a dark, hard path,
Instead of in the light.

He has made my skin and flesh grow old,
Besieged me, and has broken bones,
Surrounded me with bitterness and hardship,
Walled me in, so I can't escape.
He weighs me down with heavy chain,
Shuts out the prayers I cry in pain,
Has barred my way with blocks of stone,
Made my paths crooked…and so I groan.

He's pierced my heart,
And the people taunt and laugh.
With bitter herbs, He's stuffed and filled me,
And caused the shafts of His quiver to enter my kidneys.
Given me gall to drink,
And broken my teeth,
Covered me with ashes,
And deprived my soul of peace.
My strength has perished,

And all I had hoped for
Has been dashed and taken away,
By The Lord.

I remember my affliction and wandering,
I remember my downcast soul within me, and pondering. . .
Hope.
Because of God's great love we're not consumed,
His mercies never fail and are brand new
Each morning.
Great is your faithfulness I say within,
Yahweh is my portion,
Therefore I will hope in Him.

It's good for a man to bear the yoke while he is young,
Bide time, work hard, and grow up strong,
And wait for Salvation quietly.
For no-one is cast off by The Lord forever,
Though He brings grief,
He will show compassion,
And His awesome love will fail us never.
And God gets no satisfaction from
Bringing grief or affliction upon anyone.

DRY BONES

(Based on Ezekiel Ch37 verses 1–15).

The hand of The Lord was on me, so I was not alone,
And by The Holy Spirit I was brought to a valley of bones.
He led me to and fro,
And I saw a great many bones,
That were dry as dry could be,
On the floor of that valley.

He asked me, "Son of man, can these bones live?"
I said, "Lord Yahweh, you know".
Then He said to me, "Prophesy over these bones".

This is what The Lord says to these bones,
"I will make breath enter you and you will groan
And come to life.
I will lay sinews on you and then some flesh,
Cover you with skin and then put breath
In you, and you will live,
Then you shall know in every cell and pore,
That I am The Lord!"

So I prophesied as I was commanded,
And as I did so, there was a noise. . .
A rattling sound, as bones came together,

Bone to bone and joint to joint.
Sinews and flesh appeared on them,
Skin covered them,
But there was no breath was in them.
Then He said to me, "Prophesy to the breath.
Then I will bring these bones alive from the dead,
The Lord will breathe into these slain
Breath from the four winds that He has made".
So I did as I was commanded and told,
And breath entered them, rushing warm not cold.
And as soon as it did, they came to life,
And stood up on their feet,
A vast army in the light.

Then He said, "These bones are the whole house of Israel.
Our bones are dried up and our hope is lost,
We are completely cut off.
But, my people, I will open your graves,
And bring you up and bring you back to the land of Israel,
And when I do not fail,
You, my people, will know that I am The Lord.
I will put my Spirit in you, and you will live,
You will settle in your own land, which I shall give,
Then you will know that I, The Lord, have spoken,
And performed it", says Yahweh.

ISRAEL WILL RISE

(Based on Micah Ch7—whole chapter)

Misery is mine!
I gather no Summer fruits from the vine,
No grapes, no figs, nothing in my hand but dirt,
And the godly man has perished out of the earth,
Not one single upright person remains,
They lie in wait and hunt each other, much to their shame.
Their hands are skilled in doing evil,
The powerful dictate what they desire—
They all conspire,
The best of them is like a brier,
The most upright worse than a thorny hedge.
The day God visits you has come,
Sound the alarm! Tell the watchmen!
Don't trust your neighbor, or any friend,
No lover, no sons or daughters, for a man's enemies
Are members of his own household and his family.

"But as for me, I will look to Yahweh.
I will wait for the God of my salvation.
My God will hear me".

Don't rejoice against me, my enemy!
When I fall, I will arise,

For The Lord will be the guiding light,
Though I sit beneath these current darkened skies.

Until He pleads my case and upholds my cause,
I will bear the deserved wrath of The Lord,
He will bring me out into the light,
And I will see His righteousness.
My enemy will see and be covered with shame,
And she will see that I am blessed.
My eyes will see her downfall's meet,
As she's trodden down like the mire of the streets.

The day for building your walls will come,
The day for extending your boundaries,
The earth will become a desolate place,
Due to its inhabitants and their wicked deeds.
Shepherd your people with your staff,
Let them feed in Bashan in Gilead
As in the days when you came out of Egypt,
And I will show them marvelous things.

Nations will see and be ashamed,
Deprived of all their power,
They will lick dust like a snake,
Come out of their dens like crawling creatures, and cower,
Afraid of God and afraid of you.

Who is a God like you, who pardons inequity?
He do not stay angry but delights to show mercy.
He will again have compassion on us,
And hurl our inequities
In the depths of the sea.

GOD'S JUDGEMENT AGAINST NINEVEH

(Based on Nahum Ch1 verses 2–10).

The Lord is a jealous and avenging God,
Who takes vengeance and is filled with wrath,
Yahweh takes vengeance on His adversaries,
And He maintains wrath against His enemies.
He is slow to anger, and great in power,
He will punish the guilty, and they will cower,
His way is in the storm and whirlwinds that beat,
And all the clouds are merely the dust of His feet.

He rebukes the sea and makes it dry,
All the blossoms of Lebanon languish and fade,
Hills melt away and mountains quake,
For He is The Creator of all things made.
The very earth trembles at God's presence,
The world and everyone who lives in it,
Who can withstand His indignation?
Who can endure His anger…fierce as a blaze that spits.
His wrath is poured out like a fire,
And the rocks are shattered before
The Almighty power and presence of Yahweh, The Lord.

Yahweh is good, a stronghold in the day of trouble,
And He knows those who take refuge in Him,

But with an overwhelming flood,
He will make a full end of Nineveh, which cannot swim.
He will pursue His foes into the darkest realm,
And affliction a second time shall not rise up or swell,
For entangled like thorns,
And drunken as with their drink,
Thay are consumed utterly, like dry rubble,
For The Lord will end whatever trouble
They plot against Him.

FOLLOWING THE NEW STAR

(Based on Matthew Ch2 verses 1-13)

Far in the East, some waiting Magi
Observed a new star in the night-sky,
They realized it was a Holy sign,
Of a special baby, who is born Divine.

They packed and left home to begin,
The journey to find and worship Him,
Who would grow up to rescue us from sin,
As God's chosen one and Heaven's King.

The Magi went to Jerusalem's palace,
To ask king Herod where this baby is,
He queried them, but they would insist
That the star that had appeared was His.

He's been born The King of The Jews!
The Magi excitedly told the news,
But nothing about this Herod knew,
And a jealous plan paranoidly grew.

He sent the Magi on their way,
To find out where this baby lay,
Asking them to tell him, if they may,
The house in which this infant stayed.

The Magi followed the star that rose,
Which led them with a Holy glow,
To Bethlehem's small, dusty roads,
Where The Christ slept in a humble abode.

When the star stopped, the magi jumped for joy!
So eager to come and see the boy,
Who would break the curse and sin destroy,
So eternal peace we can enjoy.

And there with Mary lay Heaven's treasure –
God made flesh. . .grace without measure,
The magi worshipped Him with pleasure,
Before presenting their Earthly treasures.

Gold, frankincense, and myrrh was brought,
Gifts for The Savior they had sought,
Then, in a dream, the men were taught
To avoid king Herod and tell him nought.

PREPARING THE WAY

(Based on Matthew Ch3 verse 1-end of chapter)

John the Baptist came,
Preaching in the wilderness of Judea, saying,
"Repent, for the kingdom of Heaven is at hand!"
And people came to hear him from all over the land.
And John was the one
Of whom Isaiah had spoken—
The forerunner to Christ, whom God had blessed,
The voice of one crying in the wilderness,
To prepare the way for the Lord,
And make His paths straight.

John's clothes were made of camel's hair,
And his waist had a leather belt around there,
His food was locusts and wild honey,
And people thought his appearance was strange and funny.
But many went out to the wilderness to hear him,
Confessed their sins,
And were baptised by him,
In the River Jordon.

John saw many of the Sadducees and Pharisees
Coming to where he was baptising. . .
"You offspring of vipers!" he said to them,

As he felt his righteous temper rising,
"Who warned you to flee from the wrath to come?
Produce fruit worthy of repentance,
Don't think to yourselves 'We have Abraham as our father',
For that will offer you no real defence,
For I tell you, that out of these stones God can
Raise up many children for Abraham.
The axe has been laid even now to the tree-roots,
And every tree that doesn't bear good fruit
Will be cut down and cast into the fire.

I indeed baptise you in water for repentance,
But after me comes the one who is
Much more powerful than I,
Whose sandals I am not worthy to carry,
And HE has the power to baptise,
With The Holy Spirit and with Holy fire.

His winnowing fork is in His hand,
And He will thoroughly cleanse His threshing floor,
Gathering wheat and chaff from across the lands.
His wheat will go safely into the barn,
But the chaff will suffer unspeakable harm,
And be burned up with unquenchable fire".

Then Jesus came down to The Jordon from Galilee,
To be baptised by John, who argued he
Needed to be baptised by Jesus instead!
Jesus explained and insisted,
So John did consent.
As soon as Jesus was baptised,
And rose out of the water, Heaven's skies

Were opened, and He saw The Spirit of God
Come down, descending like a dove,
And alight on Him, while a voice from above
Said, "This is my Son, whom I love;
With Him I am well pleased".

JESUS TEMPTED IN THE WILDERNESS

(Based on Matthew Ch4 verses 1-12)

At the baptism of Jesus,
The Spirit alighted on Him like a dove,
A voice from Heaven said, "I'm pleased,
This is my Son, whom I do love".
And after this, The Spirit led
Lord Jesus into the wilderness,
Where He fasted for forty days and nights,
Until The Devil came to trick and test…

"If you're The Son of God", he said,
"Then tell these stones to turn to bread!"
But Jesus replied in authoritative tone,
"It is written: Man shall not live on bread alone,
But on every word that is spoken from the mouth of God".
And The Son stayed strong.

The Devil decided to tempt again,
And took Jesus to the holy city and then,
Set Him on the temple's pinnacle and said,
"Throw yourself down! For The Scripture says,
He will command His angels concerning you,
And up in their mighty hands they'll lift you,
You'll not strike your foot against a stone,

So do not fear, for you're not alone!"
But Jesus replied, much to Satan's distress,
"It is written, 'Do not put your Lord God to the test'".

Once more The Devil took The Lord,
And showed Him all the kingdoms of this world,
From a mountain top, shown in fullest splendour,
And proposed a deal to our Holy defender –
"All of this I will gladly give to you,
Take it in now...what a wonderous view,
All you have to do is bend your knee,
Bow down and simply worship me!"
But Satan forgot to realize,
Things of Earth do not impress God's eyes,
And Jesus didn't fall for his lies,
But instead, He cut him down to size...
"Away from me!
It's written in Scripture Holy,
To worship our Lord God and serve Him only".

The Devil then shook with rage and dread,
And hung his defeated, wicked head,
He left The Lord, and then the angels came
To attend Jesus and praise His powerful name.

TREASURES IN HEAVEN

(Based on Matthew Ch6 verses 19–22).

What is the use,
And what is the worth,
In storing up treasures for yourself on Earth?
Where moths and vermin will destroy,
Where thieves break in and steal and toy.
Rather, store up treasures in Heaven true,
That moths and vermin can't chew through,
And thieves do not break in and steal.
Only treasure in Heaven is treasure that's real.
Your heart will also be there where
Your treasure is. . .for your God is there.

THE HOUSE ON THE ROCK

(Based on Matthew Ch7 verses 24–28)

Everyone who hears these words of mine,
And puts them into practice will be wise,
Just like the man who built his house upon the rock,
In order to withstand any shocks. . .
The rain lashed down,
And savage winds blew,
The floods rose up,
But in this stormy view
The house was safe,
The house, it didn't fall,
Because its foundation was strong
On the rock and kept it standing tall.

But everyone else who hears these words
And ignores them, thinking them quite absurd,
Is like a foolish, lazy, ignorant man,
Who built his house upon the sand,
On the soft and shaky, shifting land. . .
When the rain lashed down,
And savage winds blew,
The floods rose up,
What did this house do,

That was built on the ground with no solid view?
It fell down with a mighty crash,
And that was that.
All that was left was rubble, fit for the trash.

JOHN THE BAPTIST IS BEHEADED

(Based on Matthew Ch14 verses 3–13).

Herod the tetrarch had arrested John,
Bound him and put him in a prison-cell strong,
Due to his brother Philip's wife—
Herodias, for John said it wasn't right,
Or lawful for him to have her,
And so he wanted to kill John in a fit of anger.
But Herod was afraid because
The people considered John to be a prophet of God.

On Herod's birthday, Herodias's daughter danced
For the guests, and thrilled Herod was so entranced,
That he promised with an oath to give her whatever
She asked for, so she went off to consult her mother.
Prompted by Herodias, the daughter returned and said,
"I want John the Baptist's severed head,
Here on a dish! That's what I wish".

The king was distressed,
But could not protest,
Especially not in front of his guests,
So he granted the young woman's gruesome request.
In prison John was beheaded,
And the head was brought,

On a platter, and given to the girl who'd sought.
    She carried it to her mother before
    John's body was buried, by his disciples,
    Who then travelled to tell Jesus, Lord.

JESUS WALKS ON WATER

(Based on Matthew Ch14 verses 22–34).

Jesus made the disciples get into the boat,
And go on ahead of Him to the other side,
While He dismissed the crowd of five thousand,
Who had been fed by God and were now satisfied.

Jesus went up by Himself on a mountain to pray,
Meanwhile the boat was a distance away,
Buffeted by the waves and winds,
And the disciples were stressed and restless within.
Shortly before dawn, Jesus walked to the boat,
Across the water, and the disciples thought it was a ghost!
They cried out in fear, for could not understand,
How He could stride on the lake as if it was just dry land.

But Jesus said, "Take courage! It is I. Don't be afraid".
Peter said, "If it IS you Lord, tell me to come on the waves
To you".
"Come" said Jesus,
And Peter obeyed.

Peter got out of the boat,
Walked on water and stayed sure and afloat,
But as he came towards Jesus, he heard the winds roar,

Was foolish, and took his eyes off of The Lord,
And because of the doubting thoughts he did think,
Quite quickly, Peter began to sink.
"Lord, save me!" he cried,
Panic swelling deep inside.

Immediately, Jesus reached out His hand,
Caught hold of Peter, saved him, and helped him to stand.
"You of little faith", He said,
'Why did you ever doubt?'
And He helped the struggling Peter,
Who by now was quite worn out.
When they climbed into the boat,
The stormy winds and waves died down,
"You are truly The Son of God",
Said all those in the boat,
And they worshipped Him aloud.

THE TRANSFIGURATION

(Based on Matthew Ch17 verses1–10)

Jesus took Peter, James, and his brother John,
Up a mountain by themselves,
There He was transfigured before them...

His face shone bright, just like the sun,
His garments became as white as the light,
And then there appeared before them Moses and Elijah—
What an amazing sight!
A bright cloud covered them,
And a voice from within
Said, "This is my beloved Son,
In whom I am well pleased. Listen to Him".

The disciples fell, face down,
Terrified upon such Holy ground,
But Jesus came,
Touched them, and said "Don't be afraid".
And when they looked up, all they saw was The Son,
And everything else they had seen and heard was gone.

As they came down the mountain,
Jesus instructed them and said:
"Don't tell anyone what you saw,
Until The Son of Man has risen from the dead".

A CAMEL THROUGH THE EYE OF A NEEDLE

(Based on Matthew Ch 19 verse 16–27).

A man asked Jesus, "Good teacher,
What good thing shall I do, that I may have eternal life?"
He didn't realize that the answer
Would cause him quandary, stress, and strife.

"There is only One who is good" Jesus said,
"But if you want to enter into life, keep the commandments. . .
You shall not murder, or commit adultery,
Honour your father and mother, and do not steal,
Love your neighbor as yourself,
And don't give testimony which isn't true or real".
"All these I have kept", the young man said,
"What do I still lack?"
He was puzzled inside his head.
Jesus told him to sell all his possessions and then,
Give it to the most needy and poorest of Men,
And he will receive great treasure in Heaven,
And THEN he could follow Jesus,
And be one of the brethren.

But the young man had enormous wealth,
And prized this over his spiritual health,
And so he turned away quite sad,
For he was unwilling to give up the Earthly fortune he had.

"It is hard for someone who is rich
To enter the Kingdom of Heaven", Jesus said,
"It's much easier for a camel to go through
The eye of a needle instead!"

When the disciples heard this, they asked—quite amazed,
"Well Master, who is it then that can ever be saved?
Jesus looked at them and said,
"With man this is impossible,
But with God all things are possible".

THE OIL LAMPS OF THE TEN VIRGINS

(Based on Matthew Ch25 verses 1–14).

At that time the kingdom of Heaven will be like
Ten virgins, who went to meet the bridegroom one night,
With their lamps...
Five were foolish,
And five were wise—
Five took their lamps, but no oil,
But the five who were wise
Brought jars of oil along,
With their lamps,
So they could keep their flames going strong.

The bridegroom was a long while coming,
And the women grew drowsy and tired,
So they all fell asleep for a while.
At midnight the cry rang out,
To let everyone know that the bridegroom was now about,
"Come out to meet him!" went the shout.

All the virgins woke up quick,
Checked their lamps and trimmed the wicks,
The foolish ones then said to the wise,
"Give us some oil, for our lamp's flames are going to die!"
"No", said the wise,

Adding to their reply—
"There may not be enough for us and you,
So here's what we suggest you do,
Go to those who sell the oil and buy some".
They did,
But while they were on their way,
The bridegroom arrived and took the five wise away,
For they were ready, and they were prepared,
So they went to the wedding banquet,
And the door was shut and locked there.

When the foolish five
Later arrived,
"Lord, Lord", they fussed,
"Open the door for us!"
But the bridegroom replied,
That they couldn't come inside,
"Most certainly I tell you, I don't know you".

"Watch therefore, for you don't know the day nor the hour
In which The Son of Man is coming".

THE SHEEP AND THE GOATS

(Based on Matthew Ch25 verse 31-end of chapter).

When The Son of Man comes in His glory,
And all the holy angels with Him,
He will sit upon His righteous throne,
With every nation gathered before Him,
And He will separate the people,
As a Shepherd parts goats from the sheep,
The goats will go on His left,
But the sheep will go on His right,
To go onwards into His precious keep.

"Come, blessed of my Father, inherit the Kingdom
Prepared for you from the foundation of the world".

The King will say to those on His right,
"Do not fear, don't be stressed,
Come you who are blessed,
By my Father,
Take your great inheritance,
Prepared for you by my Holy hand,
since the creation of the world began.
For when I was hungry,
You gave me something to eat,
When I was thirsty,

You gave me drink for my dry throat's heat,
When I was a stranger,
You invited me in,
And you gave me clothes, when I had nothing.
When I was ill,
You showed me care,
When I was in prison,
You came to visit me there".

Then the righteous will ask,
'Lord, when did we do this?'
The King will reply—
"Understand in my eyes,
Whatever you did for others,
One of the least of these sisters and brothers
Of mine, you also did for ME".

But those on His left,
Will be cursed and bereft,
And told "Understand and see,
And depart from me,
Go into the fire,
Prepared for The Devil and his angels to breathe.
For when I was hungry and thirsty,
You gave me nothing,
When I was a stranger,
You turned your back on me,
When I was in prison,
You did not visit,
And you did not clothe me
When I really needed it,
When I was ill,

You didn't care.
They will ask Him,
Lord, when was this and where
Did we not help you?
And He will reply,
It's true,
Whatever you did not do
For one of the least of these,
You also did not do for ME".

Then on that fateful day,
The goats will go away,
To eternal punishment,
Where all demons play.
But the righteous sheep,
Will find life, light, and peace,
In The King's eternal, gracious keep.

DENIAL

(Based on Matthew Ch26, verses 31–36, & 69-end of chapter)

After having The Last Supper, Jesus and the disciples went
To the Mount of Olives, where a sombre Christ turned around to them and said,
"This very night you will all fall away on account of me, for it is written:
"I will strike the shepherd, and the sheep of the flock will be scattered",
As if a wolf has bitten.
"But after I am raised up, I will go before you into Galilee".
But Peter replied HE would never fall away and refuted it quite passionately.

"Most certainly I tell you," Jesus answered,
"That tonight before the rooster crows,
You will disown me three times",
But Peter still declared in faithful tones,
"Even if I must die with you, I will not deny you!"
And the others said the same,
But when Jesus was arrested,
The disciples all fled in fear, much to their shame.

Peter was sitting outside in the courtyard,
When a servant girl came up and said,
"You were also with Jesus, the Galilean!"
But he denied it all and shook his head.

Then Peter went out onto the porch,
And somebody else saw him and said,
"This man also was with Jesus of Nazareth",
But he swore an oath against it and shook his head.

After a little while, those who stood by went up to Peter again to say,
"Surely you are also one of them, for your accent surely gives you away".
"I don't know the man!" Peter cursed and swore,
And denied this truth 'til his throat was sore.

Immediately, the rooster crowed.
And poor Peter realized that he HAD disowned
The Christ, three times, just as Jesus said.
Peter went out. . .wept bitterly. . .and held his head.

THE MAN LOWERED THROUGH THE ROOF

(Based on Mark Ch2 verses 1–13).

Jesus once again entered Capernaum,
And when the people heard that He had come,
They gathered in such large numbers that
No room was left inside,
Outside,
Or even on the welcome mat!

As Jesus preached the word to them,
A paralysed man, being carried by four other men,
Arrived,
And they tried to get inside,
To meet Jesus,
In the hopes that He would heal
This paralysed man,
For they believed His power was real.

But they could not get near,
They could not get in,
So the men looked for another way to get their friend in.
They dug through the roof,
And made a large opening,
Lowered the man down on his mat,
Their hearts faithful and hoping.

When Jesus saw their great faith,
And the paralysed man's state,
He said "Son, your sins are forgiven you".

Now, some of the teachers of the law were there,
And thought that Jesus had just blasphemed, without a care!
For who can forgive sins but God alone?
Immediately, Jesus knew
In His spirit,
These teacher's doubting views,
And questioned why they thought these things…
"Why do you reason these things in your hearts?"

He said, "Which is easier?
To say to this paralysed man,
Your sins are forgiven,
Or say to him, if you can,
Get up, take your mat,
Stand tall and walk.
I want you to know, I'm not just talk,
I am The Son of Man,
And I have authority on
The Earth to forgive sins all day long".

So, He turned to the man and said,
"I tell you, get up, arise, and lift your head,
Take your mat and go to your house".
And the man DID stand up!
He immediately rolled his mat,
In full view of them all,
And moved through the crowd,
Walking out and walking tall.

Everyone was amazed,

And praised

God, saying "We have never seen anything like this at all!"

LEGION

(Based On Mark Ch5 verse 1–18)

Jesus and His disciples,
Had travelled in a boat, across the sea,
To the region of the Gadarenes.
And when they stepped ashore,
A man with an impure spirit came
From the tombs to meet the Lord.
This man lived within the tombs,
And no-one could bind him anymore.

Often this man had been chained by hand
And foot, but he had torn
The chains apart and broke the irons
On his feet, so they could not be worn.
No-one was strong enough to subdue him,
And night and day he would cry out,
Among the tombs and hills and cut himself
With stones, and scream and shout.

When the man saw Jesus from a distance,
He ran in front of Him, bowed, and fell on his knees,
And pleaded at the top of his panting lungs,
"In God's name do not torture me!
What do you want with me Jesus,

Son of the Most High God?"
The man did shout,
For Jesus had already said to him,
"Come out of this man, you unclean spirit, come out!"
Then Jesus asked him, "What is your name?"
He replied, "We are many. . .my name is Legion",
And he begged Lord Jesus again and again,
Not to send them out of the region.
A large herd of pigs was feeding,
About two thousand up on the nearby hillside,
The demons begged Lord Jesus to send them
Among the pigs and go into them to hide.
He gave them permission to do so. . .
The unclean spirits came out and went into all the swine,
The herd promptly rushed down the steep bank,
Into the sea and were drowned, in a short space of time.

Those tending the pigs ran off to report
This extraordinary thing that had happened,
When people went out to see Jesus,
They saw the man was calm, and they were stunned,
And all the people were quite afraid,
For Legion was sitting, dressed, and in his own right mind,
Then they pleaded with Jesus not to leave them yet,
And would He stay with them if He had the time?

JESUS HEALS A SICK WOMAN

(Based on Mark Ch5 verse 24–35)

A large crowd was pressing around Jesus,
And a woman who had been bleeding for twelve long years,
Had suffered at the care of many doctors,
Spent all that she had, but the bleeding didn't clear,
Instead, she grew worse every day,
And when she heard that Jesus was coming,
She thought if she could just touch His cloak,
His Divine power would finally stop her blood running.

So, she came up behind Him in the throng,
And managed to touch the hem of His cloak,
Immediately her bleeding stopped,
She was freed from her suffering. . .it wasn't a joke.

At once, Jesus realized that power had gone out of Him,
And He turned to the crowd,
"Who touched my clothes?" He asked,
Viewing the people and looking around.

The woman, knowing what happened to her,
Came forward, trembling, and fell at His feet,
Told Jesus the entire truth,
And that her excessive bleeding had now ceased.

"Daughter, your faith has made you well,
Go in peace and be cured of your disease",
So the woman hurried off,
Pleased and relieved she had been
Cured from terrible bleeding all the while,
And finally, she had some peace.

HIS NAME IS JOHN

(Based on Luke Ch1 verses 5-67)

In the time of Herod, the king of Judea,
There was a good priest who was named Zechariah,
His wife was Elizabeth, a descendent of Aaron,
They were old and both childless because Elizabeth was barren.
Both observed God's commandments and decrees blamelessly,
They were righteous in God's sight and served Him most faithfully.

One day Zechariah in his priestly duties went
To the temple of The Lord, ready to burn the incense,
The worshippers assembled and were praying outside,
Unaware that an angel appeared to Zechariah inside.

Zechariah was startled and became gripped with fear,
But the angel reassured him and told him quite clear,
That his prayer had been heard, and he would have a son,
And that God has commanded that his name will be John.
Many will rejoice at his birth just because
He'll be great in the sight of our mighty Lord God,
He'll be filled with The Spirit even before he is born,
And will bring many people of Israel back to The Lord.

Zechariah was uncertain, for he was an old man,
His wife was old too and he was unsure they can
Have a baby at their age? He was quite confused,
But the angel was adamant he'd been sent with this news.

Because Zechariah didn't seem to believe,
Angel Gabriel said that his speech would be relieved –
Zechariah would be mute until God's appointed time,
At the birth of this John, via God's plan Divine.

Meanwhile, the people outside were wondering why
Zechariah was taking so long there inside,
And when he came out, he couldn't even squeak,
But had to make signs, for was unable to speak.
When he went home his wife Elizabeth did indeed fall
Pregnant, with their son, at the will of The Lord.

When the young virgin Mary was pregnant as well,
She visited Elizabeth, whose baby could tell
That inside of Mary was a special baby boy,
And he leaped in her womb, and both were filled with joy!
Elizabeth was filled with The Holy Spirit graciously,
And said, "Why should the mother of my Lord come to me?"

In due course, Elizabeth gave birth to her son,
Her kin shared her joy at what The Lord God had done,
Everybody assumed that the child would be named
Zechariah, but Elizabeth said that's not God's way –
"He is to be called John" Elizabeth announced,
They looked to Zechariah to confirm and pronounce,
He asked for a writing tablet and there he wrote on
Nothing but these four words . . . "His name is John".
Everyone was astonished, especially when
Zechariah's tongue was freed, and he could speak again!
Immediately he praised God, and the people could see
That The Lord was with John, and questioned what he would be.

MARY'S WONDERMENT

(Based on Luke Ch1 verses 26–56)

Father, I worship you in reverence,
For via The Holy Spirit you have sent
   A precious gift to grow in me –
   The Son of God, as a tiny baby!

Lord, I was troubled and afraid,
   On that day when the angel came,
   To tell me this astounding news,
But I am your servant, and trust in you.

I'm awestruck, Lord, just so amazed,
And my soul cries out to you in praise,
   I'm humbled and will always be,
For you have done such great things for me.

Your mercy extends through generations,
You've brought down rulers of great nations,
   To lift the humble up instead,
   Ensuring the hungry have all been fed.

You honour the promises you have made
   To our ancestors in yester days,
   For you are a faithful, loving Lord,
Who gives souls hope and makes spirits soar.

When I greeted my cousin Elizabeth,
She sensed my child is special and blessed,
Her own babe leapt inside her womb,
At the knowledge our Savior will be born soon!

I'll deliver the great deliverer of all –
Messiah, who redeems us from Hell's fall,
I can't understand why you've chosen me,
But I pledge to serve you faithfully.

And the angel said my son's birth-name
Will be Jesus, for it means "God saves",
It's wonderous, Lord, that in your grace,
I shall get to kiss His Divine face.

THE SHEPHERDS

(Based on Luke Ch2 verses 8–19).

There were shepherds living out in the fields,
Keeping watch over their flocks by night,
When suddenly and angel of The Lord
Appeared, amidst a glorious, Holy light.

The shepherds were terrified,
But the angel said, "Don't be afraid,
For I bring to you great news. . .
Today, in the town of David,
There's a Savior who's been born to all of you.
He is Christ The Lord,
And you will find
This babe, so small yet so Divine,
Wrapped in cloths and lying in a manger".

Suddenly, a great company of
The heavenly host appeared, all praising God,
This was a lot for the shepherds to take in,
But they were keen to meet The Savior of all sin.
And so, when all the angels had left,
They said to one-another, "Come on let's
Go to Bethlehem, and see this thing
Which The Lord has told us about. . .
The new-born King".

So they hurried off, and found Joseph and Mary,
And there in a manger was the precious baby.
When they had seen,
And they believed,
The shepherds spread the word,
About what had occurred,
And where they'd been.
And everyone was amazed at the shepherd's story,
And marvelled at God's grace and glory.

JESUS PRESENTED IN THE TEMPLE

(Based on Luke Ch2 verses 25–39).

There was a man in Jerusalem called Simeon,
Who was righteous and devout,
The Holy Spirit had revealed to him
That his life on earth would not run out
Until he had seen The Lord's Messiah.
Simeon went into the temple courts,
Because he was moved by The Holy Spirit,
Mary and Joseph then brought baby Jesus
To the temple, to do the law's custom within it.

Simeon took Him in arms praising God, saying—
"Now you are releasing your servant, Master,
According to your word, in peace;
For my eyes have seen your Salvation,
Which you have prepared before the face of all peoples;
A light for revelation to the nations,
And the glory of your people Israel".
Jesus's parents marvelled at what was said about Him,
And with Simeon beaming, he turned to bless them.

There was also a prophet—Anna, who was very old,
Who never left the temple, but worshipped night and day,
And would constantly fast and pray.

She came up to them at that very hour,
And in awe of The Lord's great goodness and power,
Gave thanks to God and spoke about
The child, to all who looked to the redemption
Of Jerusalem.
And Anna's joy and praise did not run out.

A SINFUL WOMAN WASHES JESUS'S FEET

(Based on Luke Ch7 verse 36-end of chapter).

A woman who led a sinful life,
Learned that Jesus would be dining that night,
At the Pharisee's house.
So she went there with a jar of perfume,
And entered into the reception room,
As she stood behind Jesus at His feet,
She felt overcome and began to weep,
Her tears did wet Lord Jesus's feet,
And still she couldn't help but weep.
The woman wiped the tears away,
With her own hair and didn't know what to say,
She simply kissed her Redeemer's feet,
And poured the perfume on them, which smelled so sweet.

The Pharisee thought if Jesus was a prophet,
He'd know what this woman was—
A sinner!
But Jesus taught him about great debt, love and forgiveness,
Turned to the woman,
And comforted her emotional distress.

"Do you see this woman?" Jesus said,
Addressing the Pharisee,

"You didn't give me water for my feet,
But the very hair upon her head,
She uses to wipe the tears she weeps,
That wet my feet.
You did not kiss me,
But this woman, from the time I entered,
Has never ceased from kissing my feet.
You did not put oil on my head,
But instead,
This woman has poured perfume on my feet,
Which smells so sweet.
Her great love for me has been shown".

"Your sins are forgiven", Jesus said to her.
The other guests began muttering to one another,
"Who is this who even forgives sins?"
Jesus said to the woman,
"Your faith has saved you. Go in peace".
So now grateful tears the woman did weep.

THE GOOD SAMARITAN

(Based on Luke Ch10 verses 29–38).

Who is my neighbor?
Jesus replied...

A certain man was going to Jericho from Jerusalem,
When he was attacked by brutal robber-men,
Who beat him and stripped him of his clothes,
And left him half-dead, at the side of the road.

A priest happened to be going down that same road too,
Saw the man hurt at the side,
But crossed over and simply walked on by.
So too, a Levite, when he came to the place,
Saw the man hurt at the side,
But crossed over and simply passed him by.

But another man—
A Samaritan,
As he travelled along, came across this man,
Was moved with compassion, and didn't walk on by,
Instead, he poured on oil and wine,
And bandaged his wounds,
Then put him upon his own donkey.

He brought the man to an inn,
And took good care of him.
When he had to leave,
He paid the innkeeper to tend
To the man, whilst he did heal and mend.
"look after him", he said,
"When I return, I will reimburse you,
For any extra expense you may have gone through".

Which of these do you think was a neighbor to this man,
Who fell into the hands of the brutal robber-clan?
"He who showed mercy on him", the expert in the law replied.
Jesus nodded and instructed him,
"Go and do likewise".

WARNINGS AND ENCOURAGEMENTS

(Based on Luke Ch12 verses 1–13).

Jesus began to speak to His disciples first,
Not the vast crowd who did eagerly thirst,
He warned them to be on their guard against
The yeast of the Pharisees,
Which is hypocrisy.
But there's nothing concealed that God doesn't know,
That won't be disclosed,
Nor hidden that will not be made known,
For what people say in the quiet and dark,
Will be heard in the daylight,
And its truth shown up stark.
And what people whisper in the ear in inner rooms,
Will be proclaimed from the housetops' highest rooves.

Jesus went on,
I tell you my friends, do not be afraid of those
Who kill the body and then can do no more. . .
Rather, fear Him who,
Once your life is through,
Has authority to throw you into Hell.

Are not five sparrows sold for two pennies?
Yet not one is forgotten by God. . .no, not any.

Indeed, the very hairs are numbered on your head,
Don't be afraid, for God has said
You're worth more than many sparrows.

Jesus said, whoever publicly before others does acknowledge me,
I also will acknowledge before the angels of God.
But whoever denies me before others openly,
Will themselves be denied before the angels of God.
And all who speak a word against
The Son of Man and causes offense,
Will be forgiven.
But anyone who blasphemes against
The Holy Spirit, and causes this ONE offense,
Will NOT be forgiven.

When you are brought before synagogues, rulers and authorities,
Do not worry about how you will defend yourselves properly,
For The Holy Spirit will lead the way,
Guide and teach you at that same hour what you should say.

THE RICH FOOL

(Based on Luke Ch12 verses 15–22)

Jesus spoke to the crowd,
And with this message He stresses -
"Beware! Keep yourselves from covetousness,
For a man's life doesn't consist
Of the abundance of the things which he possesses".

There's the parable of a rich man,
Who had yielded an abundant harvest,
He thought to himself, what shall I do?
For he didn't know how to store it best...
He had no place—no barn big enough
To store all his grain and other crops.

He then decided that he would tear
His old barns down,
And build much bigger ones there,
And then his surplus would be quite safe...
Grain for plenty of years, hoarded up in this place.
He was planning on take his life nice and easy,
He would eat lots and drink lots and be quite merry,
The rich man felt a sense of pride,
And worldly satisfaction swelled up inside.

But God had very different plans,
For that very same night He did demand
The life of this rich man.
God said to him,
"You foolish one, tonight your soul is required of you.
The things which you have prepared—Whose will they be?
So is he who lays up treasure for himself,
And is not rich toward God".

THE LOST SON

(Based on Luke Ch15 verse 11 to end of chapter)

Jesus once told a parable of a man with two sons,
"Father, give me my share of the estate", said the younger one,
So he divided his property between them and watched
The youngest son set off with all that he'd got.

He went to a distant country, and there he spent everything,
Squandering his wealth on fine times and wild living,
But then came a famine in that entire country,
And he began to be in need, where once he'd had plenty.
So, he hired himself out, and his boss sent him to
His fields to feed pigs, and the son's hunger grew,
To such an extent that he so longed to fill
His stomach with the pig's pods, or even their swill.
But no-one gave this man a single thing to eat,
So, one day he saw sense and he leapt to his feet. . .

My Father's hired servants even have food to spare!
Here I am, starving to death! So, I shall return there,
Go back to my Father, where I'll say to him true:
"Father, I have sinned against heaven and sinned against you".
I am no longer worthy to be called your son,
Make me like one of your servants, I know I've done wrong.
So, he rose, went to his father, not expecting to see
How glad and excited at his return he would be,

For even when the son was a long way off,
His father ran to him, hugged him, and kissed him lots,
For he was full of compassion towards him.

The son said to his father what he had planned to say,
Not knowing if he'd be forgiven, or be turned away,
But the father told his servants to bring the best robe,
Put a ring on his finger and sandals on his toes,
"Bring the fattened calf and kill it and we'll all celebrate,
For my son who was dead, is alive again, and this is great!
He was lost and is found!"
It was such a happy day,
Meanwhile, the eldest son came home, having worked the fields all day. . .

When he got near the house, he heard music and dancing,
So he asked a servant for the cause of the merriment and prancing,
"Your brother has come", the servant replied,
"Your father's celebrating, for he has him back, safe, sound, and alive".
The eldest son got angry and refused go in,
So his father came outside and pleaded with him,
But he answered, annoyed,
"All these years I have slaved
For you, and your orders not once disobeyed,
Yet you never gave me even a young goat to eat,
To celebrate with my friends. . .now your son gets a feast,
With the fattened calf you killed for him, now he comes home,
Having squandered your property, and now not a penny he owns!"

"My son," said the father, "You are always with me,
And all that is mine is yours, but we must celebrate gladly,
Because your brother was dead, and is alive again,
He was lost and is found",
And this healed his father's pain.

THE RICH MAN AND LAZARUS

(Based on Luke Ch16 verse19-end of chapter).

There was a rich man dressed in purple,
And fine linen, who lived every day
In luxury, while outside his gate,
A poor beggar man named Lazarus laid,
Covered in sores, and longing to eat the just the scraps,
That fell from the man's table and his guest's fine laps.
Lazarus's position was so dire and poor,
That even the dogs came over to lick his sores.

The time came when the beggar died,
And the angels carried him up to Abraham's side.
In due course, the rich man also died,
But he didn't go up to Abraham's side,
Instead, he found himself on Hell's deep, dark slide.

The rich man squirmed in agony, down in Hades,
In torment, he looked up anxiously,
And saw Abraham so far away,
Lazarus by his side,
So he cried out to say,
"Father Abraham, have mercy on me,
And send Lazarus that he may dip the tip of his finger
In water and cool my tongue!
For I am in anguish in this flame".

But Abraham refused this request,
And replied to the rich man's groans and protests,
Pointing out that a great gulf is fixed in place,
And no-one from either side can go over this space,
So nobody from Hades
Can cross over to Heaven,
And nobody from Heaven
Can cross over to Hades.

So the rich man then begged Abraham
To let Lazarus visit his family, to warn them
That there IS a Hell, and he is in it.
For he didn't want his kin to suffer the same,
And end up with him in this place of torment and pain.
Abraham said "Let them listen to Moses
And the Prophets instead".
"No", said the rich man; "If someone from the dead,
Goes to them they will repent".
Abraham said, "If they don't listen
To the Prophets and to Moses,
They'll not be persuaded,
Even if someone rises from the dead, in front of their noses".

JESUS HEALS TEN MEN WITH LEPROSY

(Based on Luke Ch17 verses 11–20)

Jesus travelled along the border between Samaria and Galilee,
When ten men who had leprosy
In a village, stopped at a distance,
Calling out to Him in a loud voice,
"Jesus, Master, have mercy on us!"
They hoped to heal them would be His compassionate choice.

When Jesus saw them, He said "Go and show yourselves to the priests".
As they went, they were cleansed,
Much to their joy and relief.
One of them came back, praising God with voice aloud,
Threw himself at Jesus's feet, for he was humbled, not proud,
Even 'though the man was a Samaritan,
And therefore classed "a foreigner" amongst these other men.
Jesus asked, "Weren't the ten cleansed? But where are the nine?
Is it just you who returns to give thanks to The Divine?"
Then He said, "Get up and go on your way. Your faith has healed you".

THE COMING OF THE KINGDOM OF GOD

(Based on Luke Ch17 verse 22-end of chapter)

Then Jesus said to His disciples,
The time is coming when you'll long to see
One of the days of The Son of Man,
But this will not and cannot be,
You will not see it, 'though certain people will tell,
"There He is!" or "Here He is!"
But it's not true and just a trick of Hell.
So don't go running after them,
For they are simply disillusioned men.

For The Son of Man upon the day
He does arrive and comes back again,
Will appear quite clear,
So the world will see and fear.
There'll be lightning flashes in the sky,
In a way that cannot be denied
That this truly is The sure Divine sign.
But,
First, He must suffer many things,
And be rejected by this generation,
Before it is shown that He IS The King.

Just as it was in days gone by,
With Noah, when the sun still shined,
People ate and drank and took no notice at all,
Until the flood arrived, and torrential rain did fall,
And destroyed them all.
But Noah was already in the ark,
For he had obeyed God's instructions and warning so stark.

It was the same in the days of Lot,
People eating, drinking, trading and planting plots,
But the day Lot left,
Sodom was made bereft,
Fire and sulphur rained down from Heaven,
And destroyed them all,
Causing the whole city's downfall.

It will be like this on the day The Son
Of Man is revealed, and then no-one
Who's on the house-top with possessions inside
Should go down to get them.
Likewise, no-one in the field should go back for anything,
Because there'll be no need or use for mere earthly things.

Remember Lot's wife?
Whoever tries to keep their life
Will lose it.
And whoever loses their life,
Will then preserve it.
On that night, two people will be in one bed,
One will be taken, and the other one will be left.
"Where Lord?" they asked,
He replied, "Where the body is,
There the vultures will also be gathered together".

THE PHARISEE AND THE TAX COLLECTOR

(Based on Luke Ch18 verses 9–15)

Jesus spoke this parable,
To some who thought their own righteousness was incomparable,
And everyone else they despised, and looked down upon...

Two men went to the temple to pray,
One a Pharisee, the other a tax collector that day,
The Pharisee stood alone to pray by himself,
Thanking God that he wasn't like anyone else,
Such as robbers, adulterers and even this tax collector...
I fast, I tithe, and know I am so much better!

The tax collector stood away at a distance and beat his breast,
Wouldn't look up to Heaven, but looked down instead,
Asked God to have mercy on a sinner like me,
And The Lord was moved by such a humble, heartfelt plea.

"I tell you", said Jesus,
"The tax collector, and not the Pharisee
Went home justified before God,
And with that one alone, He was greatly pleased".

For all those who exalt themselves,
Will be humbled for sure,
And those who humble themselves,
Will be exalted by The Lord.

ZACCHAEUS

(Based on Luke Ch19 verses 1–11).

Jesus entered Jericho, as was simply passing through,
A wealthy tax collector name of Zacchaeus was there then too,
He wanted to see Jesus, but he could not see above the crowd,
Because he was a short man,
But he was also keen, not proud,
And so he ran ahead and climbed a tree,
For Jesus was coming that way, you see.

When Jesus, Son of Man and Son of God,
Reached the spot where tax collector Zacchaeus was,
He told him to come down immediately,
For He wanted to stay at his house!
How Zacchaeus welcomed Him, gladly and eagerly.

All the people saw this and began to mutter. . .
"He has gone to the home of a sinner for supper!"
But Zacchaeus stood up and said to The Lord,
"Here and now I give half of my goods to the poor,
And if I have cheated anybody out
Of anything,
I'll pay back four times the amount".

Jesus said, "Today salvation has come to this house",
Because this man is a son of Abraham too.
"For The Son of Man came to seek and to save the lost".
And Zacchaeus was left blessed through and through.

ON THE RIGHT SIDE OF THE CHRIST

(Based on Luke Ch23 verses 39–43)

The thief hanging on the right,
At Golgotha, next to Jesus Christ,
Fell on God's unfailing grace,
And turned his dying, pain-filled face,
Asked Jesus, professing honest faith,
If He would please remember him
When He came into His kingdom.

The thief couldn't fold his hands to pray,
Yet Jesus heard his heart that day,
The thief had nothing else to offer,
Yet Jesus saved him a seat at His wedding supper.
The thief had no fine clothes,
Yet Jesus gave him righteous robes,
The thief paid no tithes,
Yet Heaven would still let him inside.
The thief admitted his crimes,
And threw himself on the mercy of The Christ,
And Jesus replied,
"Today, you will be with me in Paradise".

WATER INTO WINE

(Based on John Ch2 verses 1–12).

Jesus, His disciples and His mother
Had been invited to the wedding of another,
When Mary said to Him, "They have no more wine".
"Why do you involve me?" came Jesus's reply,
"My hour has not yet come".

But He instructed the servants to fill six jars,
With plain water, up to the brim,
Take it to the ruler of the feast,
And when they did deliver it to him,
He didn't realize that this now fine wine
Was once just water, transformed by hands Divine.
But the servants knew.

"You have saved the best wine 'til now!"
The ruler of the feast told the bridegroom.
And what Jesus did in this wedding celebration room,
By turning water into wine,
Was just the first of many miraculous signs,
Through which He revealed His glory in.
And all the disciples believed in Him.

NICODEMUS

(Based on John Ch3 verses 1–16)

Nicodemus was a Pharisee who came to Jesus at night.
He called Jesus "Rabbi",
And "a teacher come from God".
But one thing Jesus said to him, Nicodemus found quite odd. . .
"Most certainly I tell you, unless one is born anew,
He can't see God's Kingdom".
"How can someone be born when they are old?"
Puzzled Nicodemus asked,
"Surely they cannot re-enter their mother's womb,
Be born a second time—that is an impossible task!"
Jesus explained about being born of water and The Spirit,
Flesh giving birth to flesh,
But The Spirit gives birth to spirit.
Everyone must be born of The Spirit.

Just as Moses lifted up the snake in the wilderness,
So The Son of Man must be lifted up,
And those who confess
And believe,
May have eternal life in Him.

THE WOMAN AND THE WELL

(Based on John Ch4 verses 1-42)

Jesus had to travel through Samaria,
Where He came to a town called Sychar,
Jacob's well was there. . .He sat by it,
As He was tired and had walked so very far.
The noon-day sun was high in the sky,
When a Samaritan woman came to draw
Some water, and Jesus spoke to her,
She spoke back, not knowing that He was The Lord.

"Will you give me a drink?" Jesus said to her,
"How can you ask ME for a drink?" was her reply,
For Jews and Samaritans don't associate,
And they would usually just pass each other by.
"If you knew the gift of God", Jesus answered,
"And who it is that asks you for a drink,
You'd have asked Him, and He would give you living water".
The woman stopped to think.
Confused, she said, "Sir, you've nothing to draw the water with,
And this well is deep.
Where can you get this living water from?"
For she wanted some to keep.

Jesus answered, "Everyone who drinks this water,
Will surely be thirsty again,

But whoever drinks the water I give to them,
Will never thirst. . .and actually then,
The water that I give them will become in them a wonderous spring,
Of water, welling up to eternal life".
Then the woman's hope started to sing.

"Sir, please give me this living water", she said,
"So I won't be thirsty and then have to keep
Drawing water from this ordinary well",
For the strain was clear and the well, so deep.

"Go, call your husband and then come back",
Lord Jesus told her patiently,
"I have no husband", she replied,
And looked away quite shamefully.
"You are right!" Jesus said to the woman,
"In fact, you've had five husbands in the past, haven't you?
And your current man is not your husband,
What you have just said to me, is indeed true".

"Sir, I perceive that you are a prophet", she said,
"Our ancestors worshipped upon this mountain,
But you Jews claim that the place where
We must worship is actually Jerusalem".
Jesus replied that the time had now come
To worship The Father in The Spirit and in truth,
And that THEY are the worshippers God wants,
And that Salvation is from the Jews.

The woman said, "I know The Messiah is coming.
When He comes, He'll explain everything and then we'll see".
The Jesus declared, "I, the one who is speaking to you. . .
I am He".

The woman left her water jar,
And went running back to the town,
Urging the people to come and see Jesus –
He could be The Messiah,
So they came across the ground.
"He told me everything I ever did!"
The woman announced, giving testimony,
They asked Him to stay, which He did, for two days,
And due to His words, many more did believe.

THE HEALING AT THE POOL

(Based on John Ch5 verses 1–16).

In Jerusalem near the sheep gate was a pool,
Where disabled people would lie—
The blind, the deaf, the lame and the paralysed.
One invalid had been there thirty-eight years
When Jesus saw him,
And this question hit the man's ears...
"Do you want to be made well?"

"Sir," the invalid replied,
With emotion swelling in his eyes,
"I have no-one to help me into the pool,
When the water is stirred,
While I'm trying to get in,
Someone else steps in first".

Then Jesus said to him, "Arise,
Take up your mat and walk".
At once the man was cured,
And did indeed pick up his mat and walk!

The Jewish leaders said to the man,
"This is the Sabbath. You think you can
Carry your mat?

The law forbids such acts!"
But he replied, "The man who made me well,
Said "Take up your mat and walk".
So they asked him who this fellow was,
With whom he'd had this experience and talk.
The man didn't know,
For Jesus then did go,
And slipped into the crowd.

Afterwards, Jesus found him at the temple,
And said to him; "Behold, you are made well.
Sin no more, so that nothing worse happens to you".
The man went away,
And told the Jewish leaders,
It was Jesus who had made him well that day.

JESUS PROMISES THE HOLY SPIRIT

(Based on John Ch14 verses 15–18).

If you love me, keep my commands,
And I will ask The Father to help you stand,
And He will give you another advocate who
Will be with you forever, and will help you through—
The Spirit of Truth.

Because it neither sees Him nor knows Him,
The world cannot accept Him,
So it will choose to reject Him.
But YOU know Him, for He lives with you,
And will dwell inside you, so you can feel it's true.

THE VINE AND THE BRANCHES

(Based on John Ch15 verses 1–9).

My Father is the gardener,
And I am the true vine,
He takes away every branch in me
Which bears no fruit Divine,
Whilst every branch that DOES bear fruit,
He prunes, to encourage new growth-shoots,
Then it will be more fruitful than ever before,
For great is the wisdom and care of The Lord.

I am the vine,
You are the branches.
If you remain in me and I in you,
You'll find there's nothing you can't do.
You'll bear much fruit.
But apart from me you can do nothing,
If you DO NOT remain in me,
You're like a branch that's thrown away quite quickly,
And withers...such branches are picked up,
And tossed into the fire, where flames lick up,
And leave them burned.
I hope this lesson has been learned.

"In this my Father is glorified, that you bear much fruit;
And so you will be my disciples".

JESUS SENTENCED TO BE CRUCIFIED

(Based on John Ch19 verses 1-23)

Then Pilate took Jesus and sent Him to be flogged,
The soldiers clothed Him in a purple robe, and then they spat and mocked,
As they made a twisted crown of thorns to place upon His head,
Inflicting more pain and torture, although He already suffered and bled.

Once more Pilate came out to the Jews gathered there,
"I find no basis for a charge against Him", he said with due care,
But when Jesus came out, they just shouted "Crucify!"
Once more Pilate said, "No basis for a charge", and he wouldn't comply.
The Jewish leaders insisted that Jesus must die,
According to their law, for He'd blasphemed and lied,
For He claimed to be The Son of God. . .and that couldn't be!
And when Pilate heard of this, he went back inside, fearfully.

"Where are you from?" He asked Jesus, who didn't reply,
"Do you refuse to speak to me? I have the power to free you or have you crucified!"
Jesus answered, "You would have no power over me, if it were not given,
The one who handed me over to you is guilty of a far greater sin."
From then on Pilate tried so hard to set Jesus free,
But the Jewish leaders shouted and refused to believe
That Jesus was innocent, and denied Him as their king,

Insisting the charges they had made were just and right to bring.
"We have no king but Caesar" the chief priest replied,
And gave Pilate no choice but to hand Him over to be crucified.

So the soldiers took Jesus, who carried His own cross,
To the place of the skull, where His life would be lost.
Two others were crucified there—one either side of Him,
And there in the middle, hung God's pure sacrifice for sin,
Above His head was the sign of His so-called 'crime'. . .
"Jesus of Nazareth, the King of the Jews",

SIMON THE SORCERER

(Based on Acts Ch8 verses 9–25).

In a city in Samaria,
For some time, was a man named Simon,
Who practised sorcery and boasted
How great he was above most other men,
And all the people, high and low, gave him attention and exclaimed,
"This man is that great power of God!"
And were amazed by all the things he'd do and say.

The people followed Simon for a long time,
But then they believed in Philip when he proclaimed
The good news of Jesus Christ's great name,
And the kingdom of God,
And both men and women were baptised.
Simon too believed and was also baptised,
And then he followed Philip far and wide. . .
Astonished when he saw miracles and great signs.

Meanwhile, the apostles in Jerusalem heard
That Samaria had accepted God's word,
And sent Peter and John to pray for new believers. . .
That The Holy Spirit would come upon them
And they'd all be true Salvation-receivers.
For up until then,
They'd been baptised only with water by men.

When Simon saw that The Spirit was being given
At the laying of the apostles' hands,
He offered them money to share this ability,
So he too could do this and feel great and grand.
Peter answered:
"May your silver perish with you, because you thought you could obtain
The gift of God with money!"
He could see that Simon's heart wasn't right,
Before God,
And told him that very night,
He'd have no part in this ministry,
And said he needed to repent of his wickedness earnestly.
For Peter saw Simon was still a captive to sin,
And was full of bitterness deep within.

Then Simon answered,
"Pray for me to The Lord,
That none of the things which you have spoken happen to me".

PHILIP AND THE ETHIOPIAN

(Based on Acts Ch8 verse 26—end of chapter)

An angel of The Lord said to Philip,
"Go South, to the desert road,
That goes from Jerusalem to Gaza".
So he started out, and before you know,
He met an Ethiopian,
Who was a very important official,
In charge of all the treasury of the queen,
And his position was considered very special.

This man had gone to Jerusalem to worship,
And on his way back, was sitting in his chariot,
Reading the book of Isaiah the prophet,
And The Spirit told Philip to approach the chariot and stay near it.

"Do you understand what you are reading?"
Philip asked, in a kind and gentle way,
"How can I?" he said,
"Unless someone explains it to me?"
And he invited Philip to stay.
They sat together in the chariot,
And Philip explained what The Bible verse means,
And using that passage of Scripture,
He told the good news of Jesus and what he had seen.

As they travelled along the road, they came to some water,
And the Ethiopian queried why
And what was keeping him from getting baptised.
He gave orders for the chariot to stop,
And Philip and him went down,
To the water, and Philip baptised him,
And when they came out of the water now,
The Spirit of The Lord took Philip away,
And the Ethiopian did not see him again,
But he went on his way rejoicing,
For he was worshipping Jesus Christ's saving name.
Philip, however, appeared at Azotus,
And continued to travel about,
Preaching the gospel in all the towns,
And proclaiming Jesus with faithful shouts.

TRIALS AND REWARDS

(Based on James Ch1 verses 2–13).

Consider it pure joy, when you face trials of so many kinds,
Because this tests your faith well,
Revealing lessons to make you strong and wise,
Lessons that unveil blind eyes,
Lessons that you couldn't have learned otherwise.

To aid with your spiritual furtherance,
The testing of our faith produces perseverance,
Which must always finish its vital work,
Despite how much it pains and hurts,
So that we may be left mature and complete,
Not lacking anything, as we move our pilgrim's feet.

If you lack wisdom, ask The Lord,
Who, without finding fault, gives liberally to all,
And it will be given to you,
Believe it's true.
Don't doubt, because the one who doubts,
Is like a sea-wave blown by the wind and tossed about,
That person should not expect to receive,
Anything from God, if they do not believe.
And they are double-minded,
Unstable in all they do,
For they don't trust the full power of God is true.

Believers in humble circumstances
Should take pride in their high position,
But the rich should take pride in humiliation,
For temporary is their wealthy station...
They will pass away like a wild-flower,
For the sun arises with scorching power,
And withers the plant, 'til its blossom falls,
Its beauty destroyed and unadmired by all.
In the same way, the rich will fade away,
Even while they go about their pursuits, their work and play.

Blessed is the one who perseveres,
Under trials, and withstands pains and fears,
Because having stood the test, that person gains
The crown of life, in The Good Lord's name,
Which He has promised to everyone who loves Him,
And to those who put nothing else above Him.

BIBLE VERSE—ROMANS CH5 V1-7

"Being therefore justified by faith, we have peace with God through our Lord Jesus Christ; through whom we also have our access by faith into this grace in which we stand. We rejoice in the hope of the glory of God. Not only this, but we also rejoice in our sufferings, knowing that suffering produces perseverance; and perseverance, proven character; and proven character, hope; and hope doesn't disappoint us, because God's love has been poured into our hearts through the Holy Spirit who was given to us. For while we were yet weak, at the right time Christ died for the ungodly".

EPILOGUE

CONTENTS—

Dressing Appropriately In the Dark | 111

When You're Feeling Down. . | 113

The Battle For Sanity | 115

I'll Deal With the Cards I'm Dealt | 118

I Know The Truth | 120

Every Grace-Filled Breath | 122

Soul-Battery | 124

Lord, Please Re-Paint Me | 125

Persevere | 128

The Light Shows Us | 130

Nobody's Perfect | 133

Tears Travel Up | 134

I'll Be With You | 136

Bit By Bit | 138

If The Dirt Could Talk | 140.

DRESSING APPROPRIATELY IN THE DARK

Down inside the gloomy caverns of my dark and poorly mind,
The illnesses and shadows wage a battle that is so unkind,
My sanity, my peace and joy lay at the mercy of these foes,
Exposed within the dank, black fog, chilled by the wind of fear which blows.

My inner-self is fighting, panicked breath is visible in the air,
A man-made weapon in her hand seems quite a useless arm to bear,
She staggers through my cranium, a small defenceless mortal, lost and weak,
The dark and shadows laugh at me, as I try to yell but only squeak.

Her dress is torn and dirty, hanging damp and clinging to her skin,
Her bare feet slip upon the slimy, rocky ground that's here within,
Her eyes are large and teary, hands are shaking due to fright and cold,
'though body isn't elderly, inner-self feels like a 90-year-old.

It then occurs to inner-self, that if she cannot fight this foe
Alone, then she must ask for help, so on her broken knees she goes,
And prays to God Almighty, hoping He will send her extra strength,
And courage, in this long, hard war, where fog and torment won't relent.

She's humble, with no self-esteem, yet faith's unwavering in The Christ,
Who rapidly responds in love and grace and sends His dazzling light,

To pierce through all the darkness and send hellish shadows creeping back,
The mental ills recoil and shrink when Holy fire destroys their black.

The Lord restores hope, joy, and peace, and provides a haven for my sanity,
No longer exposed on jet-black rock, sound mind's unthreatened and can breathe,
And Christ advises inner-self should shed her tattered human dress,
And fit herself with armour and a shield and boots of peace instead.

A man-made weapon is no use against the mind-wars that I face,
Instead, I'll wield God's faithful sword and rest safe in His power and grace,
No longer frightened of the dark, no longer fighting all alone,
My inner-self's a warrior, bold in Christ, so all's well in mind's home.

WHEN YOU'RE FEELING DOWN...

Remember, I will never leave you—
(Deuteronomy 31:8)

Remember, child, cast all your cares on me—
(1Peter 5:7 & Psalm 55:22)

Remember, that I am The Light—
(John 8:12)

Shining on the path, so you can see—
(Psalm 119:105)

Remember, I am The Lord, your God—
(Isaiah 41:13)

Remember, you're safe beneath my wing—
(Ruth 2:12)

Remember, I love you eternally—
(1 Chronicles 16:34)

And focus upon the bliss my Heaven shall bring—
(Matthew 5:12 & James 1:12)

Remember, my grace is unfailing—
(John 1:16&17)

Remember, I loved you so much that I died for you—
(Romans 5:8)

Remember, I can ease your burdens—
(Matthew 11:28)

And my promises are faithful and true—
(Psalm 145:13)

Remember, I'll stop your feet slipping—
(Psalm 66:9)

Remember, I keep your tears safe in a jar—
(Psalm 56:8)

Remember, you're always my precious child—
(1 John 3:1)

And remember, that I am never far—
(Matthew 28:20)

THE BATTLE FOR SANITY

I'm losing it,
Not choosing it,
Mind's flailing like a drowning sailor,
Shaking, quaking,
Nonsense making,
Hope's bright light now growing paler.

Beast is knocking,
Brain is rocking,
Hands tremble—panic attack is brewing,
Panic, manic,
Sinking Titanic,
Rationale not knowing what it's doing.

Clawing, gnawing,
Burrowing, boring,
Mental ills all twist and worm,
Glugging, bubbling,
Toiling, troubling,
Nightmarish shadows brew and churn.

Flaring, glaring,
Cruel, uncaring,
Insanity's choking hands creep near,
Slithering, shivering,
Dithering, withering,
Mind's misty windows can't get clear.

Crowding, drowning,
Pressure's pounding,
I can't work out my left from right,
Blind, unkind,
Now losing mind,
In this swirling mass of jet-black night.

Jeering, Sneering,
Demon's cheering,
Watching keenly as I drop and roll,
Hopeless, helpless,
Thoughts all a mess,
I fear I no longer feel my soul.

****

Rising, reprising,
Not surprising,
Lord Jesus Christ comes to my aid,
Glowing, showing,
Blowing, mowing,
Blunting every maddening blade.

Peace song He sings,
The King of Kings,
My mind realizes it isn't lost,
Reflective, selective,
Gaining perspective,
Focusing on Christ's love and cross.

Charging, barging,
Light-discharging,
The Holy Spirit's fire alights,
Not fearing, clearing,
changing the jeering,
Insanity's demons now take flight.

Scythe is swinging,
Power is ringing,
Reverberating through my bones,
Mind's all ablaze,
With Holy flames,
Reminding me I don't fight alone.

Pray and praise,
Soul and mind raise,
Their worship to our saving Lord,
Blinking, shrinking,
Squirming, slinking,
Insanity recoils, calmness pours.

Crawling back,
Retreating black,
The darkness and the shadows cede,
Faith stands strong,
With armour on,
Madness cannot win for I believe.

No enslaving,
God is saving
Me, from my warped mind's harsh grip,
Peace remaining,
Joy maintaining,
In The Lord's strength I know I won't slip.

I'LL DEAL WITH THE CARDS I'M DEALT

Trials and The Devil deal the cards,
That make my life unpleasant and hard,
Encroaching on my personal space,
And trying to read my poker-face.
Although I've tears inside,
I shall not cry on the outside,
But keep my sword and shield held high,
And stare life, defiantly, in the eye.

Trials and The Devil deal my hands,
And make sure stressful cards do land,
They wait, expecting me to fold,
Cede,
Fall to the floor, and lay there cold. . .
But I am bold,
For The Great "I AM" of old
Provides me with a long-term view,
And promises to help me through
This temporary stress and pain,
In Jesus Christ's Mighty, saving name.

Card after card,
Murkey diamonds and broken hearts,
Clubs to club me and bash and bruise each part,

Then Trials and The Devil take the spades
To dig and suit and boot me in an early grave.
Aces are high, then Aces are low,
While jokers deal their unfunny blows.

But, finally, The Devil and Trials
Get frustrated trying to bust and break me,
And get cross, watching me smile,
As I pick up each card,
With shaking, strong hands,
Deal with whatever I have,
And in faith I still stand
On The Rock,
With my God.

Trials and The Devil keep on trying,
Although they realize my faith isn't dying.
The Lord ensures that I am able
To sit at life's table,
And manage the cards,
I'm dealt, however how many or hard,
For I always have an ace up my sleeve...
The King of all Kings and The Prince of soul-peace!
I'll claim victory in Him,
Until I get to Heaven and finally win
This game, this race,
Thanks to God's support, love and unfailing grace.

I KNOW THE TRUTH

I know the truth, deep down inside,
It's just my mind that tells me lies,
It's just my flesh that twists and binds,
It's just my pain that turns me blind,
It's just this life that makes dark rise,
It's just doubt cutting with its knives,
It's just The Devil trying to thrive.

I know the truth,
It opens my eyes,
It frees the mind,
Emboldens me,
Makes soul wise,
The Truth, you see, is Jesus Christ -
Risen King, great comforter, Savior, The Light,
In whose name I withstand and fight,
Fuelled by The Holy Spirit's might,
So every lie will get a fright,
When their deception is blown and shown up bright.

I know The Truth,
I see by faith,
Hear The Shepherd's voice,
And feel God's grace.

The Truth will last eternally,
For you see,
The Truth's all around us,
And rooted in me.

The Truth makes me joyful,
The Truth makes me calm,
The Truth will protect me from any real harm.

Praise Jesus!

EVERY GRACE-FILLED BREATH

With every breath that HE's exhaling,
I feel death's fear is less impaling,
And every breath HE breathes in,
Eases the weight, of MY own sin.
With every pained and struggled gasp,
I'm loosened more from Satan's grasp,
And with each Messianic sigh,
I'm gifted hope from God most high.

With every mortal, suffering groan,
My soul's connected to His moans,
I see that Jesus, on the cross,
Relieves MY debt and pays ALL cost.
With every Holy breath HE breathes,
My faith does swell, as I believe,
At every tortured, little whimper,
My love and awe of Him grows deeper.

For with each Holy puff of air,
MY burdens ease, as does despair,
And every movement from HIS lungs,
Ensures transgressions are far-flung.
I get a sense of pain and loss,
As I watch Jesus on the cross,

I feel bad that as I breathe in,
I'm saved, by passing HIM my sin.

With every conquering gasp of air,
I feel His grace and Divine care,
And every mumbled, human sigh,
Makes my heart leap and want to cry.
I thank you, Christ, for saving me,
With every lamb's breath that you bleed,
For as you hang in victory, dying,
My soul shares in YOUR glory. . .flying.

So, thank The Lord, for Holy breaths,
That rescue us from sin's dark death,
"It is finished!", is His winning yell,
Which redeems souls from gates of Hell.
And, so, now I will use my jaws,
To sing all praises to The Lord,
So grateful that His earthly sighs,
Shout faithful promises, in love Divine.

SOUL-BATTERY

Soul-battery is always fully charged,
For the power supply is Lord Jesus Christ,
The Light,
The Life,
The Way,
The Truth,
So soul-battery is always flatten-proof.

Even when the flesh is ailing,
Mind is failing,
And emotions flailing,
Soul-battery energy stays topped-up,
For God's blessings continue to overflow cups.

'though life may drain us,
Soul-battery is never drained,
For The Maker of all Creation remains,
He's unchanged,
And faithful,
So branches stay fruitful,
Soul-battery's core strength is Divine and beautiful,
Just like the Holy source. . .
Praise The Lord!

LORD, PLEASE RE-PAINT ME

Lord, please cleanse the stain
Within my brain,
That depression's marks leave,
Time and time again.
It's polluted tides
Ebb and flow inside,
To deposit its dark silt
Far and wide.

Seaweed glints like onyx
As it tangles my thoughts,
A black kraken attacks,
And in its legs, I am caught,
My mind is a ship-wreck,
Which rots in these seas,
That depression's cold hand
Stirs up mercilessly.

Depression sticks
Like an oil-slick,
And pulls like a tar-pit.
It takes a large brush
To paint cranium black,
It blots,

It garrots,
It leaves mind tied in knots,
Causes pain
And strain
As it stains,
Sneering,
Jeering, once again.

Brain's colors have gone,
Which were there when I was young,
For depression's siren song
Erased them,
For its darkness seems too strong.

I've cried, Lord,
I've tried, Lord,
To remove this black inside me, Lord,
But I haven't the strength,
I haven't the skills,
To beat back this tidal wave
That threatens to kill.

So, Lord, please re-paint
Where depression taints,
Send a cleansing flood,
Of your grace and blood,
And slosh and wash it all away,
Don't let my head be permanently stained,
Please allow me to see the light of day,
By removing depression and mists of grey.

Please return my skull and cranium to white,
Enlighten,

Brighten,
Please shine your might in,
Make my head light,
Overrule this plight,
Help me win this fight,
And make dawn come in this night.

PERSEVERE

(inspired by Bible quote Romans 5:3–6)

It doesn't mean you're failing,
When change doesn't happen right away,
Just persevere in suffering,
For your character is matured this way,
And character produces hope,
And hope does not put us to shame,
Due to The Holy Spirit,
Who lives in our hearts in Jesu's name.

It doesn't mean you're failing,
When you find the fiery furnace hard,
Just trust the flames can't burn you,
For The Christ's with you and He's in charge.
It's okay if you struggle,
And feel like a poor, lost, wounded sheep,
For The Shepherd won't forget you,
And will carry you safely in His keep.

It doesn't mean you're failing,
When you sin, repent, and slip again,
Just try your best each and every day,
Understanding we ALL are fallen children.
The Lord forgives in His compassion,

Unfailing grace and love so true,
And even when you think you're failing,
God encourages and He still wants you.

THE LIGHT SHOWS US

(a poem largely in prose)

The harsh light of day shows up all mistakes
Made the night before...
Any merry-making and reckless drunkenness,
Bad decisions made hastily in moonlit moments,
Whilst shadows crept,
And ignorant hedonism danced seductively,
Egged on by Hell's lust,
In a dream-state of black skies
And blurry, dimly-lit party rooms.

All seems well,
Until dawn arrives.
Then the temporary superficial happiness,
The self-pleasing and self-congratulating
Quickly evaporates,
As if they are merely spilt drinks
In the heat of the Summer's midday sun.
All breakages,
Flaws,
Stains,
Darkness
And filth

Are suddenly startling,
And illuminated brightly for all to see. . .
Much to our disgust and horror.

We lay, prostrate on the cold floor,
Naked,
Aghast at our midnight misjudgements
And past faux pas.
We are left dishevelled,
In a heap of self-loathing
When self-denial is no longer a realistic option.
We are unclothed,
Regretful,
Undignified,
Retching,
Mascara running,
Vomit and lipstick smeared across dirty mouths,
Which seemingly have no self-control,
As our foul breath emits from somewhere deep within.

We squint,
We blink at the fierce daylight,
Which beats mercilessly through the windowpane,
Reflecting sharp shards of light off the wall mirror
Directly into our tired, reluctant faces.
Fingertips reach out gingerly to touch the light,
But we are unable to physically grasp it,
Only feel it's quiet, welcoming warmth
And marvel like children
As it glows gently on the skin of our outstretched hands.

Empty bottles and last night's bedfellows

Now offer no pleasure in the eye-opening morning light.
We are fully sober...
Heads and hangovers throbbing,
Regrets banging like sledgehammers against our foreheads,
Shame hanging heavy within us,
Like thick, velvet drapes.
There's nothing like a harsh wake-up call at dawn,
To stir the soul and conscience,
To rouse hindsight
And induce fresh insight.

I hope you realize by now,
This is all just a metaphor,
Of Man's life, rife with sin,
And our dark state and fall.
And that the light is THE Light—
Son of God—Jesus Christ,
Who shows up starkly and bright,
Why we all need His redeeming might.

Do you welcome the sun when it comes?
Or when The Son comes, do you run?
Turn away in denial,
And let the darkness continue to defile?

The choice is yours,
For we all face the dawn at some stage.

NOBODY'S PERFECT

Don't worry about perfection, child,
For nothing is perfect within this realm,
Except me...
My will, my word, my timing, my nature,
My blood sacrifice that saves your souls from Hell.

Mankind isn't perfect like Jesus,
And dear child, you are not Him!
You'll make mistakes,
But forgive yourself,
For I forgive you,
Don't hate yourself,
For I love you,
Accept that you're imperfect
In the things you do.
It's okay,
Just try your best each day,
Always appreciating that no-one's walk
Is perfect along my Narrow Way.

TEARS TRAVEL UP

"I have come to answer your prayers my child",
Says The Father on one lonely night,
"But I haven't said a word, my Lord!"
I reply with some surprise and fright.

"Dear child, I don't need actual words,
To understand and know how you feel!
For I listen to your heart and soul,
Which can't hide raw emotions so real.

And, did you know, my precious child,
That each single tear you ever cry,
Encapsulates a secret message,
That evaporates up, towards Heaven's sky.

Your tears are gravity-defying,
Like a pouring raincloud, but in reverse,
Each droplet floats to reach my throne,
Instead of just falling down to earth.

I keep your tears in a bottle, my child,
I keep a record of your grief and woes,
I hear each silent scream and cry,
Know you like nobody else can ever know.

So, hush now, my beloved child,

And please trust I see your circumstance,
And I will comfort, support, and guide,
Just use your faith and give me the chance."

I'LL BE WITH YOU

I'll be with you until the end of time—
(Matthew 28:20)

I'll uphold you with my hands Divine—
(Psalm 63:8)

I'll be the anchor in life's storms—
(Hebrews 6:19)

And shelter you under my wing so warm—
(Ruth 2:12 & Psalm 17:8)

I'll be with you in the furnace flames—
(Daniel 3:15–28)

Fear not. . .for I called you by your name—
(Isaiah 43:1)

I have the power to shut lions' jaws—
(Daniel 6:10–24)

And send The Spirit in with a mighty roar—
(Acts 2:2 & 1Corinthians 6:19&20 & Ephesians 3:16)

I'll be with you on your valley's walk—
(Psalm 23:4)

I can hear your heart when you can't talk—

(Romans 8:26 & 1Samuel 16:7)

I'll shepherd you to the narrow gate—
(Matthew 7:13&14 & John 10:1–5)

And my timing's perfect and never late—
(Ecclesiastes 3:1–9)

I'll be with you at your final breath—
(Psalm 48:14 & Joshua 1:9 & John 11:25&26)

And I hold the keys of Hades and death—
(Revelation 1:18)

If you've faith as small as a mustard seed—
(Matthew 17:20)

Anything is possible. . .just trust me and believe—
(Matthew 19:26)

BIT BY BIT

I'm slowly disintegrating, bit by bit,
My once happy mindset is pushed 'til it shifts,
And where content sat, is now barren and black,
Calm and peace curl and shrink, in the dark, at the back.

I'm gradually decaying now, bit by bit,
Barely recognizable from the past child who did sit,
No more carefree days and brown hair has turned grey,
And I find my life stressful and draining most days.

I'm fading away these days, bit by bit,
It's rare that my heavy responsibilities will lift,
I look. . .there's no room left inside my poor head,
To seek and find ME, in the shadows that spread.

I see myself crumbling, bit by bit,
Misery takes over and joy doesn't fit,
I know what I want, and I see what I need,
But reality points out that this can't be achieved.

I feel myself falling away, bit by bit,
Personality and essence are both dimly lit,
I'm lost in the dark, trapped in life's small, cruel cage,
Where depression and anxiety both torture and rage.

So, I try to hang on to what's left, bit by bit,

Encouraged by God, I fight on and won't quit,
For He gives me blessings and strength every day,
And helps me to cope with what life throws my way.

The Lord shares my burdens, bit by bit,
Knows my struggles, loves me still, and this gives me a lift,
For I'm not alone as my life and needs change,
And He'll renew and repurpose as self's rearranged.

I'm learning and growing now, bit by bit,
Where confusion and weakness lay, maturity sits,
And whatever may happen, it's all in God's plans,
And I'm safe, loved, and saved, in His Almighty hands.

My faith and hope increase, each day, bit by bit,
I spy Satan sneak up, so I'm keeping my wits,
For I'll never completely just fall right apart,
Flesh is weak, but The Spirit lives and roars in my heart!

I'm heading for Heaven's rest, bit by bit,
And remember this mortal life's merely a trip,
For this world isn't home. . .home is where soul belongs,
With my Jesus. . .my Savior, with saints and angel throng.

I'm starting to feel joyous, bit by bit,
Brushing off sorrow's weight and trial's cold winds that whip,
For my soul's blessed, and peaceful, and forever will be,
And that can't fade, or disintegrate, unlike mortal me.

IF THE DIRT COULD TALK

If Earth's dirt could talk,
What would it say?
Would it say The Lord created it one day?
Would it boast that God made Man from its clay?
And that we'll all return to its dust some day?

If Earth's dirt could talk,
Would it regale the tale
Of when Eve and Adam both turned quite pale,
With horror and remorse,
When they had caused
The birth of sin, with its wicked, deadly course.
The dirt remembers the serpent's smile,
It's lying tongue, and it's tempting guile,
But as punishment for its tricking ways,
God cursed the snake for the rest of its days,
To crawl on its belly and eat the dust,
Lowest of the low, squirming on the Earth's crust.

If Earth's dirt could talk,
Would it recall that night,
When Immanuel was born, in God's great grace and might?
How it looked up at the new star shining so bright,
Which showed the arrival of The King and The Light.

If Earth's dirt could talk,
Would it pluck from its mind,
The moment Jesus used it on a man who was blind?
And how He healed his affliction,
Removing his blind-at-birth condition.

If Earth's dirt could talk,
Would it think of the memories
Of Jesus walking upon it, on the roads of His ministry?
Did the dirt see His hurt in the garden of Gethsemane?
As His sweat and tears hit the ground,
When He struggled emotionally,
Asking The Father if it was His will to "Take this cup from me?"
Does the dirt remember how the disciples' dozed sleepily,
Upon it, instead of keeping watch upon The Saviour vigilantly?
Did Earth's dirt vibrate at the sound of the feet
Of a large crowd and guards marching down the small street,
Led by Judas Iscariot, who had come to betray
Lord Jesus, and let the enemy take Him away.
Did Earth's dirt listen to Peter deny
The Christ, three times, before the people that night?
And did the Earth's dirt also then listen to
Judas's remorse, when he took up and threw
The thirty pieces of silver back,
To The chief priests and elders,
When he regretted his traitorous act.

If Earth's dirt could talk,
Would it say it had seen
Judas later hang himself,
With a rope on a tree?

If the Earth's dirt could talk,
Would it speak of the day,
It saw The Lord Jesus take the world's sin away?
For the dirt held the cross, in a hole Man had dug,
And the dirt felt the suffering and the power of God,
As The Pure Lamb's blood poured,
On the ground,
Which the dirt then absorbed.

If Earth's dirt could talk,
Would it say how it shook,
When Christ Jesus died,
Before His body was took
Down from the cross.
How many rocks split,
And people couldn't believe it,
When the temple curtain tore,
Straight in two,
And the very heavens roared.

If Earth's dirt could talk,
It would stay hush and not say
What happened in The Messiah's grave,
Until The resurrection upon the third day,
(For the dirt lay there,
In the quiet, dank air).
The dirt saw the huge tombstone be rolled away,
And The Victor step-out, on that bright, hope-filled day,
Thus providing the proof He's The Life, Truth and Way.
Oh...the miracle of Calvary!
That lasts for eternity.

If Earth's dirt could talk,

Would it say that it waits,

For the time to arrive of the second-coming of Christ?

For the Earth creaks and groans,

With the weight of our sin,

And longs for the day the new promised paradise will begin.

WORD OF THANKS.

Many thanks for reading some, or all, of this book.
I humbly hope that you enjoyed it, and that it may have personally encouraged you in some small way in your own struggles and relationship with God, and that you will feel a renewed sense of excitement and drive to delve afresh into The Bible and marvel at The Lord's wonderful works and amazing grace.

Thanks and glory go to The Lord for prompting and guiding me to write this book, and for all He does for me (and all of us) on a daily basis.
I acknowledge I am nothing and can do nothing without Him. He is my strength when my own is dwindling. . .which is often, because life is challenging, and the flesh is weak! He is my wisdom when my own fails, my patience when I have none left, and my comfort and sanctuary whenever I need it.
Thanks be to Jesus Christ, The Way, The Truth and The Life, for His willing sacrifice, for being The Conquering, Risen King and for the gracious gift of Salvation to all who believe in Him.

FURTHER INFORMATION ABOUT THE AUTHOR.

Suzanne Newman is a born-again Christian who lives in England with her family. She has been writing Christian-based poetry seriously since 2016, following her cancer journey and subsequent mental health issues. Suzanne can be found on her author page on Facebook at—
facebook.com/snewmanpoetry

Suzanne currently has four other Christian poetry books published, all of which are on sale at most on-line retailers, including Amazon.
The books are titled –
"IT's NOT JUST YOU!"
"INSPIRED BY. . ."
"KINDRED SPIRITS".
"ALWAYS".

To God Be All the Glory... Always and Forever.

www.ingramcontent.com/pod-product-compliance
Lightning Source LLC
Chambersburg PA
CBHW071721090426
42738CB00009B/1833